D0930019

Ohio

BY THEME

DAY TRIPS

Cathy Hester Seckman

Adventure Publications
Cambridge, Minnesota

Dedication

For Andrea and Larry Adkins, wishing them great day trips.

Acknowledgments

For help with photos and information, thanks go to Beth Santore, Warren Hyer, Robin Webster, Brent Haynes, Carolyn and Frank Sipkovsky, Lana Grim, and LCDR Jon Benvenuto, USCG.

Cover and book design by Jonathan Norberg

Front cover photo: Hocking Hills State Park by Shutterstock

Back cover photo: Marblehead Lighthouse by Shutterstock

All photos by Shutterstock except: 30 from Central Ohio Symphony; 36 from Holtz Museum; 127 from Ken LaRock; 4, 7, 78, 176 from Cathy Hester Seckman; 139 from Steubenville Visitor Center

10 9 8 7 6 5 4 3 2 1

Ohio Day Trips by Theme
Copyright © 2018 by Cathy Hester Seckman
Published by Adventure Publications
An imprint of AdventureKEEN
(800) 678-7006
www.adventurepublications.net

ISBN **978-1-59193-861-3 (hard cover)**; ISBN 978-1-59193-780-7 (ebook)

Table of Contents

Motorcycles Passing Pond

Ohioans believe they are at the heart of it all, and that's especially true when it comes to outdoor adventure. From the twisting motorcycle roads of southern Ohio and paddling the Muskingum River Water Trail to the Ohio to Erie bicycle trail, daytrippers have no lack of choices for adventure. Hiking at more than 70 state parks and sailing Lake Erie are also popular options. Whether you prefer the adrenaline rush of a zipline canopy tour in a state forest or a sedate wagon ride through The Wilds animal conservation center, Ohio has something for everyone.

OUTDOOR ADVENTURES

Cuyahoga Valley National Park train

1, 6 various locations in Ohio

1 Buckeye Trail

Statewide
www.buckeyetrail.org

Hikers get a little of everything on the Buckeye Trail, and exercise is only part of the appeal. By following the trail's blue blazes, you can access remote areas of wilderness to view little-seen cliffs and waterfalls. At frequent intersections with history, hikers learn about Indian mounds, centuries-old forts, and restored canal locks. Though much of the trail is through woodland and along Forest Service trails, parts of it follow country roads and even sidewalks within city limits. The 26 trail sections are divided into roughly 50-mile segments and circumnavigate the state, from Cincinnati to Cleveland and back again.

2 Caesar Creek State Park

8570 East State Route 73, Waynesville, OH 45068-9719; 513-897-3055
parks.ohiodnr.gov/caesarcreek

It was bad news for Caesar, a slave along the Ohio River, when he was captured in a raid by Shawnee Indians, but good news soon followed. The Indians adopted him and gave him a creek valley, soon known as Caesar Creek, as a hunting ground. The state park was founded in 1978, when Caesar Creek was dammed, creating Caesar Creek Lake, to control flooding on the Little Miami River. The 2,830-acre lake now boasts four public-access launch ramps, a modern marina with 124 docks, and full facilities for comfortable overnight stays. Archery, biking, camping, dog training, hiking, and swimming are popular activities at the park. A horse-friendly campground allows equestrians to take advantage of four bridle trails, ranging from 2 to 28 miles in length.

3 Cuyahoga Valley National Park

15610 Vaughn Road, Brecksville, OH 44141; 330-657-2752
www.nps.gov/cuva/index.htm

Ohio's only national park stretches from Cleveland to Akron along the winding and scenic Cuyahoga River. Hiking and biking the Towpath Trail, where horses and mules once pulled barges, is a family-friendly activity, since an excursion train, the Cuyahoga Valley

Scenic Railroad (see page 123), runs along the same route. It's easy to hop on and off the train at different points along the trail, even if your family totes strollers, bicycles, tricycles, walkers, or wheelchairs. Sights to see include a reclaimed section of the Ohio and Erie Canal, CCC structures, a restored home, and wildlife that includes beavers, bald eagles, red and gray foxes, and herons.

Grand Lake St. Marys State Park

834 Edgewater Drive, St. Marys, OH 45885; 419-394-3611
parks.ohiodnr.gov/grandlakestmarys

Oil well derricks on a manmade Ohio lake? Believe it or not, Grand Lake St. Marys is famous for them. The first offshore oil drilling in the world took place here. For some 22 years at the turn of the twentieth century, dozens of oil well derricks dotted the lake. Since 1939, though, recreation has been the state park's primary mission on the 13,500-acre lake. The family-friendly park offers cabins and a campground, unlimited horsepower boating, all-access fishing, duck hunting, a nature center, two dog parks, trails, picnicking, and play areas that boast horseshoe pits, basketball and volleyball courts, mini golf, and playground equipment.

Mohican State Park

3116 State Route 3, Loudonville, OH 44842; 419-994-4290
parks.ohiodnr.gov/mohican

The Clear Fork of the Mohican River flows through this popular park and is a great spot for river sports. On any summer weekend, convoys of floating, roped-together tubes are a common sight. There's one for Mom, one for Dad, more for each kid, another for the dog, and, of course, one for the picnic cooler. Colorful kayaks swish through gentle rapids while novices in rental canoes learn the basics on the user-friendly river. Hiking, bicycling, and bridle trails crisscross the park. A particularly challenging mountain biking and hiking trail loops 24.5 miles around a gorge. The trail is regularly labeled one of the "best" and "must-ride" spots and is a stop on the National Ultra Endurance Series.

Motorcycling

www.motorcycleroads.com/Routes/Ohio_111.html
www.sundaymorningrides.com/road/states/OH/

The Appalachian foothills of eastern and southern Ohio are the place to be for motorcyclists who crave curves and switchbacks. State Route 555, also known as the Triple Nickel, is a popular route, stretching from Little Hocking on the Ohio River northwest toward Roseville. The Black

7, 10 various locations in Ohio

Diamond Run stitches together small towns around Wayne National Forest that were important to the area's coal heritage. State Route 170, beginning in East Liverpool and winding north to Poland, was named one of the top ten motorcycle roads in the United States by *American Motorcyclist* magazine. The Dragon's Tail coils along Route 78 between McConnelsville and Glouster, up and down the hills and back and forth through the hairpin turns known as "the twisties." State Route 147 curves through what is known as Little Switzerland, an area famous for its hilltop vistas and Amish farms.

Rallies

AMA Vintage Motorcycle Days, early July
Mid-Ohio Sports Car Course, 7721 Steam Corners Road, Lexington, OH 44904; 800-262-5646
www.amavintagemotorcycledays.com

Ohio Bike Week, around Memorial Day
5316 Milan Road, Unit 2, Sandusky, OH 44870; 419-502-0022
ohiobikeweek.com

Thunder on the Strip, autumn
Geneva-on-the-Lake, OH 44041; 440-466-1768 or 440-466-2361
thunderonthestrip.com

7 Muskingum River Water Trail

Statewide
watercraft.ohiodnr.gov/Portals/watercraft/pdfs/maps/wtmuskingum.pdf

If you're in the mood for a scenic boat cruise and the old-fashioned appeal of hand-operated locks, head straight for the Muskingum River Water Trail, which is open to recreational traffic for 112 miles, from Dresden to Marietta. In the 1800s, the Muskingum River was improved with locks, dams, and side-cut canals to connect the Ohio and Erie Canal to the Ohio River. When commerce slowed to a halt after the Civil War, the river gradually returned to recreational use, after restoration work by the U.S. Army Corps of Engineers and the state of Ohio. In 2006, the lock system became the first Navigation Historic District in the United States. It's also a National Historic Civil Engineering Landmark. Besides canal and frontier history and artifacts, boaters can investigate Underground Railroad history, as the Muskingum was a busy corridor for escaped slaves before the Civil War.

Muskingum Watershed Conservancy District

1319 3rd Street Northwest, New Philadelphia, OH 44663; 877-363-8500
www.mwcd.org

The 10 reservoirs of the district were created to prevent flooding and help native wildlife, but for sportsmen, they mean premier fishing and boating opportunities, drawing large crowds of boaters and campers. But there's much more here. Do you like moonlight kayak tours? Fishing tournaments? Boat races? Beach parties? All of them are scheduled throughout the year. Eight of the lakes have campgrounds, and there are nine marinas among them. An equestrian camp and a trail system that connects to Malabar Farm State Park are available at Pleasant Hill Lake Park, and a state water trail is in the works. All of the parks have numerous hiking trails. Tappan Lake serves as regional headquarters for the Buckeye Trail Association.

Ohio Power ReCreation Land

www.aep.com/environment/conservation/recland/
740-962-1205

What does a power company do with a strip mine when all the coal is gone? Well, American Electric Power reshaped the land and planted 63 million trees. Then they built a 60,000-acre recreation area. It features 6 campgrounds, 40 miles of bridle trails, 9 miles of bicycle trails, 24 miles of the Buckeye Trail, and 600 lakes and ponds. In all, the area spans three Ohio counties. Here you can also see what's left of the Big Muskie, once the largest earth-moving machine ever built. Its "bucket," or scoop, sits at Miners' Memorial Park within the recreation area (see pages 86, 89). The somewhat surprising thing about ReCreation Land is that everything is free. All you need to visit the park and use its camping and recreational facilities is a free permit, downloadable from the website, or available at the AEP office in McConnelsville or the district ODNR office in McConnelsville.

Ohio to Erie Trail

Statewide
www.ohiotoerietrail.org

If you're a bicyclist but don't want to travel on public roads, check out the Ohio to Erie Trail, which primarily follows railroad and canal routes. Besides bicyclists, the trail welcomes hikers, wheelchair users, rollerbladers, and equestrians. The trail crosses the state diagonally, connecting Cleveland, Akron, Columbus, and Cincinnati. Twenty-two regional sections make up the 326 miles of the route. The Ohio to Erie Trail sponsors an annual adventure ride that includes lodging and luggage transportation, and awards participants with a "326" sticker.

15 various locations in Ohio

11 Pymatuning State Park

6100 Pymatuning Lake Road, Andover, OH 44003; 440-293-6030
parks.ohiodnr.gov/pymatuning

One of the running jokes around campfires at Pymatuning is whether Ohio fish taste better than Pennsylvania fish. It's a legitimate question, since the 14,000-acre reservoir and surrounding park straddle the state line. Walleye and muskellunge are the ones to catch, and Ohio fish definitely taste better, whether you snag them from the deck of your pontoon, through the ice, or from the shore at your campsite. Besides boating, fishing, and swimming, visitors can trap or hunt (with firearms and bows) during the fall and winter. Campers can choose from some 350 sites on the Ohio side, or more than 50 cabins. Nesting eagles have made a home at one end of the Ohio side campground for several years, and they are best viewed from the water. Sharp-eyed birders can also spot great blue herons and red-tailed hawks.

12 Cleveland Velodrome

5033 Broadway Avenue (entrance off Pershing), Cleveland, OH 44127; 216-256-4285
clevelandvelodrome.org

If you're a bicyclist, or even a potential bicyclist, you might check out this Olympic-style velodrome track. It's a bit more than 160 meters around and has a 50-degree embankment at the corners, reducing to 15 degrees on the straight sections. You must complete a class or be certified at another track in order to use the velodrome. Private sessions and coaching are available, or you can opt for open riding or an unlimited membership. If you want to race, you have to be approved by a track official. Sanctioned races are held some Friday and Saturday evenings. A youth-development program is free but requires reservations, and there are sessions sponsored by the Boys and Girls Clubs of Cleveland. The velodrome is open May through October.

3 Wayne National Forest

13700 US Highway 33, Nelsonville, OH 45764; 740-753-0101
www.fs.usda.gov/wayne

Wildflowers and forest songbirds populate Wayne National Forest, along with plenty of native animals. You might not actually see a bobcat on the 15-mile loop in Wildcat Hollow, but be on the lookout for wild turkeys and salamanders. Outdoor enthusiasts flock to the 250,000 acres of Wayne National Forest, not just to enjoy nature, but for camping, horseback and off-highway vehicle riding, and hunting. Rock climbing and rappelling are allowed in the forest, but not encouraged. Big Bend Swimming Beach is available on Lake Vesuvius. Nine different campgrounds are scattered throughout the forest, some are walk-in only, while others offer RV sites for a reasonable fee. Both big- and small-game hunting is allowed in sections of the forest away from camping, day-use, and mining areas.

4 The Wilds

14000 International Road, Cumberland, OH 43732; 740-638-5030
thewilds.columbuszoo.org

Picture this: The sun sets over a ridgeline in the distance as you amble on horseback through wildflowers that are alive with butterflies seeking a last meal before dark. To your left is a lumbering herd of white rhinos that includes a calf. In the middle distance, two giraffes sway across the track. Tonight you'll stay at Nomad Ridge, enjoying a catered dinner at your campfire before retiring to your private yurt. After a catered breakfast, you'll visit a conservation center dedicated to the endangered eastern hellbender salamander. Are you deep in the heart of Africa? India? China? No, you're just out in Cumberland, Ohio, visiting The Wilds. Twenty-nine species are represented among the 500 animals on open ranges at this conservation center, including Bactrian camels, ostriches, cheetahs, takins, and oryx. Horseback and bus tours are available, as are a variety of camps and group events.

5 Zipline, Canopy, and Climbing/Rappelling Tours

Adrenaline junkies should head to southern Ohio for 50 mph zipline tours. Once a thrill-seeker is strapped into a harness, an overhead cable sends them zooming hundreds of feet through treetops and across rivers and lakes. Slightly less adventurous folks can opt for canopy tours that feature elevated walkways and bridges through treetops. Some companies offer "kid-friendly" ziplines for children as young as five. Additional options include moonlight zip tours and canopy walks, ground-level Segway excursions, and add-on trips to nearby attractions.

Climbing and rappelling adventures are a little harder to find, but once you get there, great fun is in store.

Adventure Rock Climb & Rappel Hocking Hills Adventure Trek
Logan, OH 43138; 740-777-2579
www.explorehockinghills.com/recreation/adventure-rock-climb-rappel-hocking-hills-adventure-trek/

Akron Fossils and Science Center Ziplining
2080 South Cleveland-Massillon Road, Copley, OH 44321; 330-665-3466
www.akronfossils.com/zip-line

Common Ground Canopy Tours
14240 Baird Road, Oberlin, OH 44074; 440-707-2044
www.commongroundcenter.org

High Rock Adventures
10108 Opossum Hollow Road, Rockbridge, OH 43149; 740-385-9886
www.explorehockinghills.com/recreation/high-rock-adventures/

Hocking Hills Canopy Tours
10714 Jackson Street, Rockbridge, OH 43149; 740-385-9477
www.hockinghillscanopytours.com

Holden Arboretum
9550 Sperry Road, Kirtland, OH 44094; 440-602-3838
www.holdenarb.org/visit/canopy-walk-emergent-tower/

Toledo Zoo and Aquarium Ziplining
2 Hippo Way, Toledo, OH 43609; 419-385-5721
www.toledozoo.org/aac

Treefrog Canopy Tours
21899 Wally Road, Glenmont, OH 44628; 740-599-2662
www.treefrogcanopytours.com

Valley Zipline Tours
3465 Duffy Road Southeast, Lancaster, OH 43130; 740-654-3392
valleyziplinetours.com

Wild Zipline Safari
14000 International Road, Cumberland, OH 43732
thewilds.columbuszoo.org/home/visit/plan-your-visit/zipline-safari-tours

Outdoor
Adventures

Horseshoe Pond, Cuyahoga Valley National Park

Chief Leatherlips Monument, Scioto Park, Dublin

The Chippewa, Erie, Kickapoo, Shawnee, and Honniasont tribes, among others, have called Ohio home for ages. In fact, the word *Ohio* itself means "large river" in the Seneca language. American Indians first arrived in Ohio more than 12,000 years ago, but by the mid-1800s, most of Ohio's populations had succumbed to introduced diseases or had been forcibly displaced to reservations in Kansas and Oklahoma. Today, American Indians once again live in Ohio, and evidence of just how profoundly American Indians influenced the state abounds—from the state's place names, earthworks, and historic sites to American Indian culture's many historic and contemporary impacts on Ohio's history, literature, and beyond.

AMERICAN INDIAN CULTURE

1 Chief Leatherlips Monument

7377 Riverside Drive, Powell, OH 43065-9761
www.roadsideamerica.com/story/9791
www.wyandotte-nation.org/culture/history/biographies/leatherlips/

When Ohio schoolchildren learned about Wyandot Chief Leatherlips'
place in Ohio history, everyone giggled over the name, but it's actually a tragic story. As a chief, he encouraged peace with European
settlers, going so far as to sign the 1795 Treaty of Greenville, which
ceded most of Ohio. He believed it was best for his people to coexist
with settlers. His tribe sentenced him to death in 1810, officially for
witchcraft, but actually for his political position. Leatherlips refused
to go back on his word to keep the peace, and was executed by tom-
ahawk at the command of a committee headed by his brother. He's
remembered today in a quirky monument at Scioto Park in Dublin. A
sphinx-like 12-foot head made of artfully placed limestone slabs overlooks a hillside near the site of his death. The effigy, designed and
built by Ralph Helmick in 1990, is reminiscent of the Crazy Horse
monument in South Dakota. It's possible to walk out onto Leatherlips' head for an up-close and personal look at this statue honoring
the famous peacemaker.

2 Fort Ancient Archaeological Park

6123 State Route 350, Oregonia, OH 45054; 513–932–4421 or 1–800–283–8904
www.fortancient.org

History is not only preserved here, it's palpable and accessible for
everyone from preschoolers to lifelong learners. The National Historic Landmark operates customized tours that offer classes, family
groups, and history buffs a chance to learn about the history of the
pre-Columbian Hopewell and Fort Ancient Native American cultures.
Small children are able to touch and play with natural materials used
in aboriginal daily life; older children can learn spear-throwing and
participate in scavenger hunts. Critical-thinking skills come into play
with middle-schoolers as they learn how decisions affect daily living.
Adults may be able to participate in research projects and fieldwork.

Great Serpent Mound

3850 State Route 73, Peebles, OH 45660; 800-752-2757
www.arcofappalachia.org/serpent-mound/

Building a monument wasn't so easy in pre-Columbian times. Native Americans didn't have steel or concrete to construct this serpent effigy, so they used the material they had at hand—dirt. Workers piled enough dirt to build a three-foot-high snake with an open mouth and coiled tail; altogether, it's 1,348 feet long. Three burial mounds are adjacent. Scientists speculate that the snake effigy was used for ceremonial purposes. The mound may also have been important in Native American cosmology, since its shape also is aligned astronomically. Visitors today can come up with their own theories, as they walk the paths around the mound and visit the nearby Serpent Mound Museum.

Hopewell Culture National Historical Park

16062 State Route 104, Chillicothe, OH 45601; 740-774-1126
www.nps.gov/hocu/index.htm

We learn a lot about the history of America in school, but what was life like here before Europeans arrived? The Scioto River Valley in southwest Ohio was a busy place for Native Americans 2,000 years ago. People of the Hopewell Culture flourished there, leaving behind mysterious and monumental earthen enclosures. Six separate groups of earthworks are preserved and partially rebuilt in this historical park surrounding Chillicothe: High Bank Works, Hopeton Earthworks, Hopewell Mound Group, Mound City Group, Seip Earthworks, and Spruce Hill Earthworks. Five are open to the public, where visitors can see reconstructed mounds and learn about the social, spiritual, ceremonial, political, and economic lives of the Hopewell people. The park's visitor center, at the Mound City Group just north of Chillicothe, includes artifact exhibits and information about tours.

Leo Petroglyphs & Nature Preserve

Park Road, Ray, OH 45672; 800-600-0144
www.ohiohistory.org/visit/museum-and-site-locator/leo-petroglyphs

Ancient American Indians not only built massive earthworks in Ohio, they produced art that has survived for millennia. This tiny preserve in south-central Ohio consists of a half-mile trail that leads inquisitive hikers along a sandstone gorge and past small waterfalls to a rock shelter. Here, people of the Fort Ancient culture drew dozens of petroglyphs that include human figures and footprints, plus images of birds, fish, and animal tracks.

6 various locations in Ohio

6 Powwows

Music, color, regalia, food, and heritage combine to educate and entertain visitors to a powwow. Performers with Native American heritage provide a thrilling and inspiring spectacle that serves to remind us all of the rich and complex history of America's first inhabitants.

Many powwows begin with a grand entrance parade. Some include contests in drumming, dancing, singing, and storytelling; others are noncompetitive. It's worthwhile to attend just to see the dancers' regalia. Women and men typically perform separately in traditional, ceremonial, and modern forms, including the Hoop Dance, Gourd Dance, Snake Dance, and Bread Dance. Some powwows are intertribal, while others are sponsored by just one or a few tribes. There may be a charitable component, with proceeds going to a local food pantry or worthy cause. Veterans are honored guests.

AuGlaize Village Powwow & Gourd Dance
AuGlaize Village & Farm Museum, 12296 Krouse Road, Defiance, OH 43512
www.calendar.powwows.com/events/4th-annual-auglaize-village-powwow-gourd-dance/

Baby Bison Days
Boss Bison Ranch, 45701 Unionvale Road, Cadiz, OH 43907; 740-942-8726
www.calendar.powwows.com/events/baby-bison-days-2017/

Great Mohican Pow-wow
Mohican Reservation Campgrounds & Canoeing, 23270 Wally Road, Loudonville, OH 44842; 800-766-2267
www.mohicanpowwow.com

Harvest Moon Gathering
The Ridge Museum, 14430 Flint Ridge Road, Glenford, OH 43739; 740-787-2869
www.calendar.powwows.com/events/harvest-moon-gathering-pow-wow/

Healing Mother Earth Powwow
Evergreen Lake Park, 703 Center Road, Conneaut, OH 44030; 440-536-2213
www.calendar.powwows.com/events/healing-mother-earth-9th-annual-powwow/

Hocking Hills Powwow
26792 US Highway 33, Rockbridge, OH 43149; 330-423-3990
www.calendar.powwows.com/events/hocking-hills-ohio-pow-wow/

Honoring Our Ancestors: 13th Annual Intertribal Powwow
UELN & Ashtabula County Antique Engine Club, 4026 US Highway 322, Williamsfield, OH 44093; 440-536-2213
www.calendar.powwows.com/events/honoring-ancestors-13th-annual-powwow/

Honoring Tradition: An Eastern Woodland Native American Celebration
Fairfield County Fairgrounds AAA Building, 157 East Fair Avenue, Lancaster, OH 43130;
740-304-9720
www.calendar.powwows.com/events/honoring-traditions-eastern-woodland-native-american-celebration/

Keeping the Tradition Powwow
Sunwatch Indian Village, 2301 West River Road, Dayton, OH; 937-268-8199
www.calendar.powwows.com/events/keeping-tradition-pow-wow/

Moccasin Trail Powwow Gathering
Atwood Area Fall Festival
Atwood Lake Park, 9500 Lakeview Road Northeast, Mineral City, OH 44656;
330-343-6780
www.atwoodfallfest.org

Monroe Powwow
Monroe County Fairgrounds, State Route 26 North, Woodsfield, OH 43793;
740-934-9353
www.calendar.powwows.com/events/monroe-pow-wow/

Native Woodland Gathering
Hall–Fawcett Park, 4595 County Road 153, Zanesfield, OH 43360; 937-441-1565
www.calendar.powwows.com/events/8th-annual-native-woodland-gathering/

Region of the Moundbuilders Powwow
Everett Park, 170 Everett Avenue, Newark, OH 43055; 740-443-5560
www.calendar.powwows.com/events/region-of-the-moundbuilders/

Spirit of the People Gathering
Soaring Eagle Retreat, 375 Horner Chapel Road, Peebles, OH 45660; 937-302-9624
www.calendar.powwows.com/events/spirit-people-gathering/

Ohio Bird Sanctuary, Mansfield

As free and wild as songbirds and raptors appear, they can be frighteningly dependent on us for their very existence. An owlet in a contaminated habitat, a hawk that's been struck by a car, or even a human-raised crow may never be able to survive unprotected. They remind us of our responsibility to nature and its inhabitants. Birds are protected statewide in nature preserves, where daytrippers may also catch glimpses of other wildlife, including coyotes, deer, turkeys, reptiles, and amphibians. Some preserves are known for their geological features, others for their profusion of wildflowers. Still others protect original forests, wetlands, and prairies. Most feature hiking trails that allow visitors to enjoy nature without disturbing delicate ecosystems.

BIRDS, NATURE, AND MORE

1 Black Swamp Bird Observatory

13551 West State Route 2, Oak Harbor, OH 43449; 419-898-4070
www.bsbo.org

If you've ever thought you might like to dip a toe into the birding world, Black Swamp is the place to start. Your first excursion might be a walk along the modest 1/3-mile birding trail behind the visitor center. If you're intrigued by the migrant songbirds there, or the peculiar antics of the American woodcock, your next step is a Birding for Beginners workshop, held periodically at the Observatory. After that, you'll be interested in Hike the Dikes, monthly guided excursions into Magee Marsh and the Ottawa National Wildlife Refuge to view birds and local flora and fauna. Scheduled boat excursions on Lake Erie might also interest you, along with a once-a-year field trip to see wintering raptors at Killdeer Plains. Research, education, and conservation are the missions of the Observatory, and enthusiastic birders and volunteers are always welcome.

2 Clifton Gorge State Nature Preserve

2381 State Route 343, Yellow Springs, OH 45387; 614-265-6561
www.naturepreserves.ohiodnr.gov/cliftongorge

You might imagine canyons are only found out west, but we've got them right here in southwest Ohio. Clifton Gorge, one of 136 State Nature Preserves in Ohio, is also one of 23 National Natural Landmarks in the state. Set amid 268 acres along the Little Miami River, the Gorge is a spectacular example of the ways in which glacial rivers cut through limestone and dolomite bedrock. In this case, geologists speculate that glacial "potholes" (lakes left behind by melting glacier ice) may have connected to form one especially deep and narrow channel. Sections of rapids and waterfalls are visible from the trail along the Little Miami River. The Gorge trail is especially known for spring displays of snow trillium.

Crabill Fen State Nature Preserve

Buck Creek State Park, 1901 Buck Creek Lane, Springfield, OH 45502; 614-265-6561
naturepreserves.ohiodnr.gov/crabillfen

Crabill Fen, named for a pioneer family, is a spring-fed alkaline wetland at the edge of the Kennard glacial outwash. There are no visitor facilities or trails, but nature lovers will find it worthwhile for the unusual plant species preserved there. These include prairie dock, limestone savory, fen Indian plantain, fen sedge, and blue-leaved willow, among others. Ecological management, including removal and treatment of invasive species, keeps the fen protected. Because the fen is a sensitive area, access is by downloadable permit from the ODNR Division of Natural Areas and Preserves; request at least 14 days in advance.

Crawford Park District

2401 State Route 598, Crestline, OH 44827; 419-683-9000
www.crawfordparkdistrict.org

Two parks, three nature preserves, a wildlife area, and a bikeway make up this park district serving Crawford County in northern Ohio. The 53-acre Unger Park has a 3-mile trail system that includes sections open to horses from June through October. Yearly prescribed burns keep the restored prairie healthy. Unger also features more than 100 species of reintroduced prairie plants and a pond and wetland habitat. Lowe-Volk Park near Crestline has 2 miles of trails, a fishing dock, and a boardwalk. Sears Woods State Nature Preserve is known for abundant spring wildflowers, songbirds, and wood frogs. Heckert Nature Preserve is known for butterflies, some of which overwinter there. The 33-acre Daughmer Prairie Savannah preserves a remnant of unplowed, deep-soil land, with species including prairie cord grass, Bicknell's sedge, wheat sedge, and flat-stemmed spike-rush. At the Sandusky Wildlife Area, a yearly drawing allows a limited number of hunters from Crawford County. The Colonel Crawford Bikeway, 32 miles long, winds through several parks and preserves. One stop is at a monument that honors Col. Crawford, captured and killed by Native Americans in 1782.

Lake Katharine State Nature Preserve

1703 Lake Katharine Road, Jackson, OH 45640; 740-286-2487
www.naturepreserves.ohiodnr.gov/lakekatharine

Lake Katharine is one of the little-known gems of southwest Ohio. Surrounded by a 2,019-acre preserve, the wildflower display here includes native orchids and both bigleaf and umbrella magnolias. The western side of the preserve is closed to visitors, but elsewhere, Calico Bush, Salt Creek, and Pine Ridge trails are available to hikers. The 6 miles

of trails lead visitors across creeks, through marshlands, and under the edges of massive sandstone cliffs. The 120-acre artificial lake is open only to permit holders for a fee. Those seeking to use the lake can call the park office on certain days of the month to request a permit. Five per day are issued Fridays through Mondays between April and October, sunrise to sunset. Limited hunting is sometimes permitted in the preserve.

6 Mud Lake Bog State Nature Preserve

Northwest Township, Williams County
naturepreserves.ohiodnr.gov/mudlakebog

This unique kettle-hole lake is bordered by an alkaline fen on one side and an acidic sphagnum bog on the other. The combination must be good for insect life, since many dragonfly and damselfly species thrive here, including the lilypad forktail, marsh bluet, Canada darner, and mottled darner. Some of the 26 plant species found at Mud Lake Bog are swamp birch, shrubby cinquefoil, and lesser bladderwort. Because the 74-acre bog is a sensitive area, access is by downloadable permit from the ODNR Division of Natural Areas and Preserves; request at least 14 days in advance.

7 Ohio Bird Sanctuary

3774 Orweiler Road, Mansfield, OH 44903; 419-884-4295
www.ohiobirdsanctuary.com

If you get past the "ick" factor, get a cup of mealworms at the visitor center before you tour the sanctuary. The aviary residents will appreciate it. Besides songbirds in the aviary, raptors and vultures unable to survive in the wild are housed in outdoor cages. You might even see wild vultures visiting their protected kin. The 90-acre sanctuary is home to some 52 species of migratory and resident birds. Outdoor aviaries are wheelchair and stroller accessible. Four miles of hiking trails wind through the preserve, including a wheelchair-accessible boardwalk on the Wood Duck Trail. The sanctuary does educational outreach and offers field trips and nature camps for student groups. The educational building is available for corporate retreats and meetings, parties and celebrations, and even weddings.

Ohio Wildlife Center

6131 Cook Road, Powell, OH 43065; 614-734-9453
www.ohiowildlifecenter.org/

At the Ohio Wildlife Center, amphibians, reptiles, small and large mammals, raptors, turkeys, waterfowl, and migratory birds find homes when they can no longer live in the wild. Outreach programs, day camps, Scout programs, and guided tours introduce visitors to the varied wildlife at the center. A regular lecture series is offered to the public and covers such topics as drinking water safety, bees, nocturnal animals, tree identification, and more. Historic Bonner Barn, originally built in 1891, provides space for 100 people to celebrate weddings and family events, hold meetings or retreats, or just throw a party. The center is not open daily, so be sure to check their schedule before visiting. They are generally open to the public the second Sunday of the month, from noon to 2 p.m.

Scheick Hollow State Nature Preserve

Laurel Township, Hocking County
naturepreserves.ohiodnr.gov/sheickhollow

Black Hand sandstone, known for forming sheer cliffs and gorges throughout Ohio, surrounds narrow, fern-filled Sheick Hollow, which is home to hemlock, birch, and Canada yew. Seasonal waterfalls provide a cool environment for rare nesting birds that attract bird-watchers. Green warblers found here include magnolia, Canada, and black-throated species. Hermit thrushes and solitary vireos can also be spotted. The hollow and its floodplain are also home to a number of slump blocks (accumulated material that has slid or fallen). Access is by downloadable permit from the ODNR Division of Natural Areas and Preserves; request at least 14 days in advance.

Sheldon Marsh State Nature Preserve

2715 Cleveland Road West, Huron, OH 44839; 888-OHIOCMP
naturepreserves.ohiodnr.gov/sheldonmarsh

Along Sandusky Bay, the rare coastal wetland habitat of Sheldon Marsh provides a home, or at least a safe stopover, for some 300 bird species. In the summertime, birdwatchers can spot great blue herons, red-tailed hawks, black-crowned night-herons, wood ducks, common terns, woodcocks, and great horned owls, as well as many species of songbirds. In the spring, wildflowers spotted at the preserve include the spectacularly spiky cardinal flower, plus Dutchman's breeches and cut-leaved toothwort. Later blooms include trout lilies, trilliums,

wild ginger, and wild geraniums. The parking lot and 1-mile trail are wheelchair accessible. Hikers can access the beach from the trail system.

11 Stratford Woods State Nature Preserve

3083 Liberty Road, Delaware, OH 43015; 740-363-2548
naturepreserves.ohiodnr.gov/stratfordwoods

Two buttonbush swamps occupy the north section of Stratford Woods. Also called shrub swamps, these transitional areas are freshwater wetland ecosystems that occupy a niche halfway between wetter "true" swamps and dryer marshes. Pin oak and swamp white oak are present in Stratford's buttonbush swamps. The south section is drier, and includes Delaware limestone bedrock in a ravine. A stream in this section is festooned every spring by mayapples, dwarf larkspur, and blue phlox, among other wildflowers. The 95-acre preserve is home to more than 30 species of trees, including oak, hickory, ash, and maple. Amenities at the preserve include a parking lot, loop trails, restrooms, and an outdoor education center.

12 Whipple State Nature Preserve

1194 State Route 247, Manchester, OH 45144
www.naturepreserves.ohiodnr.gov/whipple

Geology buffs appreciate Whipple (named for land donor Robert A. Whipple) for its examples of slump blocks (material that has accumulated after falling downhill), dolomite cliffs that can rise to 30 feet, and the mysterious springs and sinkholes along a narrow ridgetop. Flower lovers are thankful for the luxurious displays of spring wildflowers and luxuriant ferns. The 448-acre preserve is available to nature lovers and hikers along 2 miles of moderately difficult loop trail. Park carefully, because space for cars is limited in the pull-off area.

Wildflowers, Clifton Gorge, Ohio

Central Ohio Symphony

Outdoor drama, ballet, symphonies, fine art, and Broadway musicals—Ohio has it all. Home to the largest theater district outside New York City, Ohio also features three outdoor dramas and numerous fine art museums. Enjoy a symphony under the stars or a ballet at venues all around the state. Whether you prefer the Renaissance masters or the most cutting-edge mixed-media artists, you can find their work in Ohio.

THE ARTS

1 Aronoff Center for the Arts

650 Walnut Street, Cincinnati, OH 45202; 513-621-ARTS (2787)
www.cincinnatiarts.org/aronoff-center

To spend a day or an evening immersed in the arts, Cincinnatians head downtown to the Aronoff Music Hall, which hosts everything from chamber music groups and ballet and dance companies to a boys' choir, opera, dance troupes, and pops and symphony orchestras. The site's Weston Art Gallery boasts exhibition spaces featuring art in all media. Education is part of the Aronoff's mission, and the center runs an "Artists on Tour" program and holds events and performances for schools.

2 Butler Institute of American Art

524 Wick Avenue, Youngstown, OH 44502; 330-743-1107
butlerart.com

The Art in the Early Morning program makes exhibits at the Butler come alive for babies in strollers (and their parents), preschoolers (and their parents), and senior citizens. The free Thursday programs allow in-depth gallery visits with a docent and include an art activity for older children. Since 1919, the Butler has collected and preserved American art of all types. The permanent collection includes pieces by Winslow Homer, Mary Cassatt, Albert Bierstadt, and Andy Warhol. The Beecher Center at the museum focuses on electronic and new media art, and includes the Zona Auditorium.

3 Central Ohio Symphony

24 East Winter Street, Delaware, OH 43015; 740-362-1799 or 888-999-2676
www.centralohiosymphony.org

From their home at Ohio Wesleyan University's Gray Chapel, the symphony's 65 professional musicians have been serving central Ohio for 37 years with the motto "Engage the Community with Music." Besides maintaining a regular concert schedule at several venues, the group hosts outreach programs that have included therapeutic drumming for vulnerable populations, a "Dreams Project" for court-involved teen girls, and Carnegie Hall's Link Up program for elementary students. A yearly Benefit in the Barn benefits local charities. The symphony is currently directed by Maestro Jaime Morales-Matos. Check the symphony's website for performance dates and locations.

Cincinnati Art Museum

953 Eden Park Drive, Cincinnati, OH 45202; 513-721-2787
www.cincinnatiartmuseum.org

Back in 1876, the ladies of Cincinnati organized an association dedicated to bringing culture to the hinterlands. Ten years later, they opened the Cincinnati Art Museum, billed as "The Art Palace of the West." Today that modest effort has come, through art, to involve full-scale community engagement. Daily tours give visitors an up-close-and-personal look at selected highlights of the museum collections. Monthly themed events welcome visitors after dark, and daytime programs include summer art camps, tours for young children, puppet shows, and more. A speakers' bureau travels through the community with programs for adult and family audiences. For digitally inclined art lovers, the museum's bimonthly podcasts cover not only art, but food, sports, and popular culture.

Living Word Amphitheatre

6010 College Hill Road, Cambridge, OH 43725; 740-439-2761
www.livingworddrama.org

The story of Jesus Christ unfolds onstage in Ohio's only outdoor Passion Play. With shows on Friday and Saturday nights through the summer months, there are also themed events like Scout Night, Biker Night, Canned Food Drive Night, 4-H Night, and Tour Bus Night, all of which fill the seats of the 400-seat amphitheatre. The authentic and colorful sets designed by Biblical dramatist Frank Roughton Harvey include the Temple, Herod's Palace, the Sanhedrin, the Via Dolorosa, Golgotha, and Christ's Tomb, and all come to life as the story unfolds. Behind the Scenes and Front Set tours precede every show. A youth and family rally is part of the summer schedule, and it features a children's day of games, crafts and lessons, interactions with animals, and food options.

Playhouse Square

1501 Euclid Avenue, Suite 200, Cleveland, OH 44115; 216-771-4444
www.playhousesquare.org
www.cleveland.com/onstage/index.ssf/2012/12/playhousesquare-area_spots_for.html
www.thechocolatebar.com

For millions of Midwesterners, Playhouse Square is within easy reach for a day trip or an overnight excursion. Choose from nine theaters, including an outdoor performance space and restored historic theaters

that date back to the Roaring Twenties. Patrons can choose from Broadway shows, music and dance, and children's performances. For student productions, the Cleveland Playhouse, Cleveland State University, DANCECleveland, Great Lakes Theater, and Tri-C JazzFest all call Playhouse Square home. Packages that include tickets, lodging, and parking are available. Before or after your show, pick out a restaurant or bistro from the dozens in the theater district. My personal favorite is the Chocolate Bar. Beyond the ubiquitous chocolate martini, you can sample hot chocolate with a kick, chocolate shooters, the dark chocolate bomb, or the ultimate wine and chocolate flight.

7 Schoenbrunn Amphitheatre

1600 Trumpet Drive Northeast, New Philadelphia, OH 44663; 330-339-1132
www.trumpetintheland.com

The first time I saw the outdoor drama *Trumpet in the Land*, I was still young enough to be open-mouthed and wide-eyed. Horses galloped across the stage, American Indians danced, rifles cracked, and tension mounted until the bone-chilling finale. Instantly, I became a lifelong fan of live theater. *Trumpet*, the premier attraction of Schoenbrunn Amphitheatre, tells the story of Moravian missionary David Zeisberger, his pioneer settlement, and the infamous Gnadenhutten Massacre, in which 96 Moravian Christian Lenape Indians were killed by Colonial militiamen, five years before the Revolutionary War. A revolving cast of actors, many of whom participate for years, is drawn mostly from the surrounding community. The amphitheatre also hosts contemporary plays throughout the summer season, as well as holiday-themed events. Bring a rain poncho, just in case, and prepare to be thrilled and chilled by the emotional and passionate story of the Ohio frontier.

8 Sugarloaf Mountain Amphitheatre

5968 Marietta Road, Chillicothe, OH 45601; 866-775-0700
www.tecumsehdrama.com

The spectacular outdoor drama *Tecumseh!* has enthralled audiences here since 1973. Live cannon fire erupts onstage, horses barrel through the water, torches ignite, and loincloths flutter as the story unfolds under the stars on summer nights. Tecumseh was a Shawnee Indian who led a large confederacy of Native Americans who wanted to keep settlers out of the Ohio country. With his brother Tenskwatawa, who was renowned as the Prophet, he fought from present-day Chillicothe to the wilds of what is now Ontario. The brothers were involved in the Battle of Tippecanoe, and in the War of 1812, when the Confederacy allied with the British. Tecumseh's death during the Battle of the Thames in Canada ended the Confederacy, which withered away thereafter.

Besides the drama, the 1,800-seat amphitheatre hosts a bluegrass concert series and performances of Shakespeare.

Toledo Museum of Art

2445 Monroe Street, Toledo, OH; 419-255-8000
www.toledomuseum.org

Walking through the glittering displays of the Glass Pavilion, you might find yourself wanting to try your hand at glass art. Could you do it? It's easy to find out at one of TMA's Glass Art Workshops. From a flashy firework paperweight to a delicate, multicolored fish, participants can unleash their inner artist and take home a one-of-a-kind, very personal keepsake. Workshops in glass are among many offered to children, teens, and adults at TMA. All the classes are linked to museum exhibits and include gallery tours. The TMA campus includes not only the Glass Pavilion but five other buildings that house an exhibition space with 30,000 works of art, a concert hall, a lecture hall, classrooms, and more. El Greco, Cézanne, Rembrandt, and Picasso are among the artists represented.

Wexner Center for the Arts

1871 North High Street, Columbus, Ohio 43210; 614-292-3535
www.wexarts.org

Adventurous art lovers will find plenty to love at the Wex. Contemporary artists working in a variety of media are showcased in the galleries of the Wexner Center at the Ohio State University. Classic, foreign, and independent film is always on tap on-site, and music, theater, dance, and lectures rotate on the Wexner stages. Artists' residencies are awarded in all disciplines. For the public, classes from filmmakers, curators, and choreographers are all available. You can attend book signings and free guided exhibition tours. For youth, there are video competitions, boot camps, social events, and a yearly family film festival.

Lou Holtz Upper Ohio Valley Hall of Fame and Museum

Ohio museums are nothing if not friendly. Generally, if it isn't behind glass or a velvet rope, you can touch it. In fact, your kids can touch it, too. Whether you like fire trucks, fine china, sports memorabilia, Civil War history, inaugural gowns, classic motorcycles, or pliers carved from a single piece of wood, we've got a museum for you.

MUSEUMS

INDUCTION
2009
CLEVELAND

Rock and Roll Hall of Fame Museum, Cleveland

1 AMA Motorcycle Hall of Fame Museum

AMA Motorcycle Hall of Fame Museum
13515 Yarmouth Drive, Pickerington, OH 43147; 614-856-2222
www.americanmotorcyclist.com/hof

One of the cooler things about this museum is the covered priority parking, right next to the main entrance, for motorcycles. Wheel your ride into a first-class spot, and stroll through the doors to immerse yourself in the history of motorcycling, much of which, surprisingly, took place in Ohio. The second-coolest thing is that American Motorcycle Association members are admitted free. Here, motorcyclists have a place where they will always feel valued and welcome. Be sure to visit the Hall of Fame itself, where famous riders like Bessie Stringfield and Malcolm Smith are remembered, along with less-famous leaders in racing, touring, trail riding, and manufacturing. In addition to rotating exhibits, dozens of classic bikes are on permanent display, including the 1894 Roper Steamer and a 1916 Harley Racer.

2 American Civil War Museum of Ohio

217 South Washington Street, Tiffin, OH 44883; 419-455-9551
www.acwmo.org

Though only a few minor Civil War battles occurred in Ohio itself, Ohio played an outsized role in the Civil War, providing hundreds of thousands of soldiers for the Union effort. This museum examines the impact of the war on the lives of the common soldier, the sometimes-anguished decisions of their leaders, and the hardships and loss suffered by those at home. Visitors can study the medicine used by field surgeons, the issues faced by prisoners, and the aftermath of America's first modern war. One story many Ohioans might not know is the role three Ohio companies played in the Great Locomotive Chase in Georgia, also known as Andrews' Raid.

American Sign Museum

1330 Monmouth Avenue, Cincinnati, OH 45225; 513-541-6366
www.americansignmuseum.org

Once upon a time, Tod Swormstedt edited *Signs of the Times* magazine. Facing a midlife crisis in 1999, he opened a sign museum inside an arts center. Still, that didn't solve the problem of what to do with his larger-than-life McDonald's and Holiday Inn signs. By 2012, the American Sign Museum had its own building. When you enter the exhibit space, you're surrounded by glowing neon, frenetically flashing signs, and more than a few oddities. See everything from beer and hardware store signs to those that once adorned pharmacies, motels, and even funeral homes. Besides the signs themselves, the museum displays motors, cabinets, and the tools and paraphernalia of a sign maker. You can even order your own custom neon sign and watch it being built onsite by Neonworks. The museum is open Wednesdays through Sundays, and hosts events as well.

Bible Walk Wax Museum

500 Tingley Avenue, Mansfield, OH 44905; 419-524-0139
www.biblewalk.us

Don't be intimidated by the idea of a Bible Walk. Religious or not, this museum is very much worth everyone's time. Set on the grounds of Diamond Hill Cathedral and framed by a peaceful garden, the Bible Walk was built in the 1980s by mostly volunteer labor and continues to expand every year. Its centerpieces are the 78 life-size wax dioramas of Bible scenes, some of which are animated. Everyone has a favorite, and mine is inspired by the 23rd Psalm. You might recognize a few of the people in the dioramas from Hollywood; the museum often repurposes wax figures it receives from other museums. You may therefore spot an old John Travolta or Tom Cruise figure standing amid the biblical scenes. There's also an extensive Christian art gallery at the museum, including oil paintings, folk art, wood carvings, and a rare-Bible collection. A dinner theater operates during the summer months.

Bicycle Museum of America

7 West Monroe Street, New Bremen, OH 45869; 419-629-9249
www.bicyclemuseum.com

If you grew up in Ohio, a state full of small towns, chances are you had a bicycle, and the rock-hard leg muscles to propel it. At this museum you can explore the history of one of your earliest sports, from velocipedes to electric bikes and tricycles to three-wheelers meant for senior citizens. Which one is my favorite? It's an interesting puzzle as you browse the collection. I'm torn between the Smith & Wesson police

bicycle, the 1860 blacksmith-built high-wheeler, and the Airstream folding bike, available only to owners of Airstream travel trailers. Or wait, would I prefer a 1998 Autobike Classic, meant for cyclists who never could figure out how to shift gears? Take your time, and let everyone in the family choose a favorite.

6 Canton Classic Car Museum

123 6th Street Southwest, Canton, OH 44702; 330-455-3603
www.cantonclassiccar.org

They surely do have cars. At this downtown museum, you can see an Ohio-built Holmes, called "possibly America's ugliest car," plus a floatable Amphicar, a 1911 Model-T Ford, a front-loading BMW Isetta, and a 1937 Packard hearse (with companion flower car), among other highly collectible vehicles. They also have steam engines, a fire truck, and thousands of pieces of automobile paraphernalia, vintage advertisements, presidential artifacts, local history items, and some unclassifiable oddities like an EX-LAX thermometer. It's the perfect museum for those who like to search out the unexpected, as well as the expected.

7 Central Ohio Fire Museum & Learning Center

60 North 4th Street, Columbus, OH 43215-2511; 614-464-4099
www.centralohiofiremuseum.com

Children are welcome visitors to the restored 1908 Columbus Engine House #16, home of the Central Ohio Fire Museum & Learning Center. Wearing kid-size fire coats, they can slide down a pole, "drive" a fire truck with sirens wailing and lights blazing, and experiment with a fire hose. Personalized tours are a big draw, not just for kids, but for their parents and grandparents. The engine house features original horse stalls, complete with hoof marks on the doors, and vintage hand-drawn and horse-drawn equipment. Meticulously appointed motorized equipment is also on display. On Fire Safety Way, visitors learn about fire prevention and safety and visit the Burned Room Display. The engine house is on the National Register of Historic Places.

Glass Heritage Museum

109 North Main Street, Fostoria, OH; 419-435-5077
fostoriaglass.com
www.glasspass.org/glassheritate.htm

Because of its abundant supplies of natural gas, Fostoria was seen as a good place for a glass factory in 1887. By the Roaring Twenties, the town had 13 of them. Some made workaday window glass, others made globes for some 60 percent of the period's kerosene lamps. The globes on display at this small museum range from heavy-handed pebbled glass to delicate three-layered prism glass. Some are heavily decorated with glass ribbons and medallions; others are ethereal white-and-silver confections with delicately floating designs. Pretty glass tableware is also on display, part of the more than 1,000 items in the museum's collection.

The John & Annie Glenn Museum

72 West Main Street, New Concord, OH 43762; 740-826-3305
johnglennhome.org

This living-history museum presents three time periods that were important in the lives of John and Annie Glenn. In alternate years, costumed docents lead visitors through the house as it appeared in either 1937 (during the Great Depression), 1944 (during World War II), or 1962 (the year Glenn orbited Earth). I visited in a 1962 year, when a docent portraying Glenn's mother Clara described the family's fear and pride in Glenn's historic achievement. On the top floor of the home are rooms full of memorabilia and information on Glenn's careers in the military, in space, and in politics. A movie on the lives of John and Annie Glenn, and a gift shop, are available in a museum addition.

Lou Holtz Upper Ohio Valley Hall of Fame and Museum

120 East Fifth Street, East Liverpool, OH 43920; 330-386-5443
www.louholtzhalloffame.com

Legendary football coach Lou Holtz didn't like the idea of a hometown museum dedicated to him and his achievements, but he did like the idea of a Hall of Fame, so a compromise was made. The historic First National Bank building became the institution's home, and the first honorees were inducted into the Upper Ohio Valley Hall of Fame in 1998. Inductees since then have included many Ohio Valley movers and shakers, as well as some nationally known names like Franco Harris, Regis Philbin, and Robert Urich. Besides information on Holtz's career, the museum features unique local history pieces, like a vintage

fire engine, a carousel horse from long-gone Rock Springs Park, and a sprawling model train setup built to look like East Liverpool.

11 Merry-Go-Round Museum

301 Jackson Street, Sandusky, OH 44870; 419-626-6111
www.merrygoroundmuseum.org

Of course you can ride the merry-go-round here. Though it's not in original condition, the Allan Herschell carousel that is the centerpiece of this museum has been restored and filled with figures both vintage and modern. Stargazer, the lead horse, keeps his head to the sky and is a popular choice for riders. The museum, opened in 1990 after a temporary exhibit proved wildly popular, features not only carousel animals but Dentzel carving tools, memorabilia, and a restoration shop where visitors can watch artisans bring carousel animals and other folk art back to life. The museum raffles a hand-carved carousel horse every year as a fundraiser.

12 Motts Military Museum

5075 South Hamilton Road, Groveport, OH 43125; 614-836-1500
www.mottsmilitarymuseum.org

It started with Civil War memorabilia that Warren Motts kept in his basement. Today, his collection fills a sprawling campus and covers many American conflicts. The museum also displays the largest collection of 9/11 artifacts outside New York City. Motts' mission is to bring to life the people behind the memorabilia. "See this uniform?" he asks kids. "Here's a picture of the guy who wore it. Here are his letters, here's his shaving kit. He's a real person." I have a personal connection to one piece of memorabilia there. Motts displays a Vietnam-era chopper, Huey Helicopter #66-17048, that was flown by a friend, former Army Warrant Officer Joe Sepesy. A videotape of Joe talking about his old bird is on file at the museum.

3 Museum of Ceramics

400 East Fifth Street, East Liverpool, OH 43920; 330-386-6001 or 800-600-7180
www.themuseumofceramics.org

Just walking up to the building, a former post office, is a grand experience. The Beaux Arts edifice, which cost $100,000 to build in 1909, features domed ceilings, antique pendant lamps, a marble and terrazzo floor, and wrought iron fixtures. The museum tells the stories of some 300 potteries that once operated in this Pottery Capital of the World. Famous pottery imprints like Taylor, Smith & Taylor; Homer Laughlin; Knowles, Taylor & Knowles; and others fill the display cases. Sturdy Rockingham and yellow ware are shown alongside delicate Lotus Ware. In the cavernous basement are displays of pottery machinery, dioramas, and activity rooms. Upstairs, a theater provides space for community activities and an introductory film on the pottery industry.

4 National First Ladies' Library

331 South Market Avenue, Canton, OH 44702; 330-452-0876
www.firstladies.org

In 1995, Canton resident Mary Regula asked First Lady Hillary Rodham Clinton why there wasn't a museum dedicated to first ladies. Clinton agreed that the idea was long overdue, and in 1998 she was the first person to access the new organization's website. Later that year, former First Lady Rosalyn Carter cut the ribbon to open the library in the former home of William and Ida Saxton McKinley. Today the library is a National Historic Site and includes an Education and Research Center nearby. The price of admission includes access to both buildings. Parking is free, but reservations are strongly recommended. Since the site operates under the National Park Service, NPS passes are accepted. The McKinley home is meticulously restored and presented in its full original glory, from President McKinley's enviable desk to the gorgeously layered period wallpaper in the front hall.

5 National Museum of the Great Lakes

1701 Front Street, Toledo, OH 43605; 419-214-5000
www.inlandseas.org

Go ahead, stand at the wheel of the *Col. James M. Schoonmaker* and close your eyes. Imagine powering through waves, fighting storms, and delivering coal to Great Lakes cities. You're the master of your universe. Then open your eyes and look through the panoramic windows of the bridge, out to the water. Can't you just see it all? You may not actually be able to sail it, but you can walk through the *Schoonmaker* at the National Museum of the Great Lakes from May through October. The museum itself, on the edge of the Maumee River, sits amid a park

20 various locations in Ohio

full of marine artifacts that preserve Great Lakes stories and history. Committed to education, the museum also hosts open houses for teachers, and has a kids' club and a speakers' bureau.

16 National Road and Zane Grey Museum

8850 East Pike, Norwich, OH 43767; 800-752-2602 or 740-826-3305
www.ohiohistory.org/visit/museum-and-site-locator/national-road-and-zane-grey-museum

Roadbuilding at the turn of the nineteenth century was a sweaty and dangerous enterprise, from felling trees by hand to shifting boulders and blasting hillsides. The construction of the National Road, also called America's Main Street, is detailed in a 3/8-scale, 136-foot diorama at this fascinating museum. Allow plenty of time for the diorama, then more time to learn about Zane Grey, a former dentist from nearby Zanesville who wrote more than 80 books. He's best known for westerns, but he is also the author of three books about his family, the pioneering Zanes, who included Revolutionary War heroine Betty Zane. Grey's study, including his original desk, has been re-created in the museum, and some manuscripts and memorabilia are also on display.

17 National Underground Railroad Freedom Center

50 East Freedom Way, Cincinnati, OH 45202; 513-333-7500 or 877-648-4838
www.freedomcenter.org

The Ohio River was, of course, an important piece of the Underground Railroad prior to the Civil War. Once across, escaped slaves were out of slave territory, but not out of danger. The Rankin family of Cincinnati, for instance, helped more than 2,000 people to freedom from their home on Liberty Hill, overlooking the river. This museum chronicles the stories of the escapees and their "conductors" along the secret, illegal "railroad" to freedom. Beyond that, the organization operates a free genealogy center and is active in the Freedom Stations Program, which links with other Underground Railroad sites. It is also involved in modern abolitionism, which works to combat worldwide slavery today. The Center also operates an Implicit Bias Learning Lab.

8 America's Packard Museum

420 South Ludlow Street, Dayton, OH 45402; 937-226-1710
www.americaspackardmuseum.org

Operating in a restored 1917 Art Deco Packard dealership, this museum is dedicated to preserving Packard history. Along with automobile memorabilia, more than 50 cars are on display, representing models from 1903 to 1958. The museum's education arm teaches schools and clubs about automobile engineering, 3D printing, and metal shaping. The museum is also an event venue, and can handle up to 250 people.

9 National Packard Museum

1899 Mahoning Avenue Northwest, Warren, OH 44483; 330-394-1899
www.packardmuseum.org

In Warren, home of the Packard, this small but nicely appointed museum features one-of-a-kind Packard automobiles, like the last-known Warren-built car—the 1927 Sterling Knight—and a 1941 One Eighty Touring limousine owned by Mrs. J. W. Packard. Several Packard Marine engines are also on display. Memorabilia include Packard banners, other period artifacts, and displays on the Packard Electric Company. Educational programs include hands-on restoration workshops, plus seminars and panel discussions.

0 Presidential Museums and Libraries

Here's another reason Ohio considers itself at the heart of it all—eight presidents have called it home. Presidential libraries and museums are thick here, and all are popular among fans of U.S. history and politics. The modest home from which James Garfield conducted his Front Porch Campaign, and the sprawling estate of Major General, Congressman, Governor and President Rutherford B. Hayes are among them.

James A. Garfield National Historic Site
8095 Mentor Avenue, Mentor, OH 44060; 440-255-8722
www.nps.gov/jaga/index.htm

James A. Garfield Monument
Lakeview Cemetery, 12316 Euclid Avenue, Cleveland, OH 44106; 216-421-2665
www.lakeviewcemetery.com/visit/points-of-interest/james-a-garfield-memorial/#.
V7bEPctOnqA

U.S. Grant Birthplace
1551 State Route 232, Point Pleasant, OH 45153; 513-497-0492
www.usgrantbirthplace.org

Warren G. Harding Memorial
380 Mt. Vernon Avenue, Marion, OH 43302; 740-387-9630 or 800-600-6894
www.hardinghome.org/harding-memorial/

Benjamin Harrison Memorial
112 South Miami Avenue, Cleves, OH 45002
www.hsmfmuseum.org

William Henry Harrison Tomb State Memorial
41 Cliff Road, North Bend, OH 45052; 844-288-7709
www.ohiohistory.org/visit/museum-and-site-locator/william-henry-harrison-tomb

Harrison-Symmes Memorial Foundation Museum
112 South Miami Avenue, Cleves, OH 45002
www.hsmfmuseum.org

Rutherford B. Hayes Presidential Library & Museums
Spiegel Grove, Fremont, OH 43420; 419-332-2081
www.rbhayes.org

William McKinley Presidential Library & Museum
800 McKinley Monument Drive Northwest, Canton, OH 44708; 330-455-7043
www.mckinleymuseum.org

William Howard Taft National Historic Site
2038 Auburn Avenue, Cincinnati, OH 45219; 513-684-3262
www.nps.gov/wiho/index.htm

21 Rock & Roll Hall of Fame

1100 East 9th Street, Cleveland, OH 44114; 216-781-ROCK (7625)
www.rockhall.com

"Sensory overload" is a frequent comment of visitors to this world-famous shrine of rock and roll. Why Cleveland? Because they fought hard for it, and they've been enthusiastically partying hard ever since. Just the groundbreaking, for instance, featured performances by Chuck Berry, Pete Townsend, and Ruth Brown. Johnny Cash, Aretha Franklin, and Booker T. & the M.G.'s came to the opening. Once a year, the Rock hosts a very loud celebration for that year's five inductees into the Hall of Fame. To date, 317 rock and roll performers and influencers have been inducted as official participants in rock and roll history. Even fans can take part in the action by renting the Rock for a wedding, prom, or party.

Warther Museum & Gardens

331 Karl Avenue, Dover, OH 44622; 330-343-7513
thewarthermuseum.com

It's a visit many Ohioans make sooner or later, because word-of-mouth draws them. "You won't believe what this guy did!" is enough to bring tourists, and they're always glad they came. Ernest Warther was a woodcarver, plain and simple, and what he did with his talent was plainly, simply, amazing. He carved in ebony, ivory, and walnut. His amazingly ornate carving of the Lincoln funeral train is probably the most famous piece, but no less amazing are the hundreds of wooden pliers scattered through the collection. He carved, and his descendants still carve, each pair from a single piece of wood. He also collected more than 5,000 Native American arrowheads, and his wife Frieda collected 73,000 buttons, which she arranged in quilt motifs all over the walls of her Button Cottage. The Swiss-style gardens are popular for events, and the museum itself offers a candlelight-dinner tour for groups.

3 Youngstown Historical Center of Industry and Labor

151 West Wood Street, Youngstown, OH 44501; 800-262-6137
www.ohiohistory.org/visit/museum-and-site-locator/youngstown-historical-center-of-industry-and-labor

Iron and steel mills are still a sore subject in the Mahoning Valley, once a thriving industrial community that has seen hard times since wholesale mill closures in the 1980s. A rich legacy survives at this museum, though. Immigration brought factory workers into the area's working-class neighborhoods, and their stories are documented in photographs and in a re-creation of a company house. The tools and clothing of steelworkers are on display. Visitors can also see reproductions of a mill locker room and a blooming mill, where steel ingots were made. Stories of the different mills' "last heats" are also told.

Edgewater Beach at sunset, Cleveland

We don't seem like a beach state, but we are. Toes in the sand, Ohioans enjoy miles of beaches along Lake Erie. We don't have much in the way of seashells, but searching for beach glass is a favorite hobby here. Clear, green, cobalt blue, seafoam, and light purple are lying around, waiting to be found. There's even a Beach Glass Festival in Ashtabula.

BEACHES AND DUNES

1 East Harbor State Park

1169 North Buck Road, Lakeside, Marblehead, OH 43440; 419-734-4424
www.eastharborstatepark.org

If you close your eyes and use your senses, you might have trouble believing you're in the Midwest. Gentle waves lap at the sand, seagulls caw, a nice breeze ruffles your hair, and sunshine pours down. Sand crunches between your toes. Children shriek and giggle, parents call out, and you can smell barbecue from the picnic ground next door. Open your eyes to see a 1,500-foot beach sprawling across the Lake Erie shoreline. Early in the mornings, walkers and joggers measure out their exercise. Families crowd the beach on sunny days, and even cloudy ones. Late at night people are still stargazing and enjoying the lakeside ambiance. The well-maintained bathrooms and changing rooms also include outdoor showers.

2 Edgewater Park

6500 Cleveland Memorial Shoreway, Cleveland, OH 44144; 216-635-3200
www.clevelandmetroparks.com

Part of the impressive Cleveland Metroparks system, Edgewater Beach boasts a new $3 million Beach House, where friends gather for a meal and drinks on the second-level deck. Down on the 2,400-foot beach, amenities include a dog-friendly area, a volleyball court, shelters, a fishing pier, and a thousand-foot swimming area. For the fitness-minded, there are kayaks and paddleboards available, and walking paths. Yoga classes start at 7 a.m. Clevelanders gather up their blankets and beach chairs on summer Thursday nights for Edgewater LIVE, a concert series with local bands. Music lovers can also take advantage of rotating local food trucks, craft beer, and beach-themed cocktails.

3 Fairport Harbor Lakefront Beach

301 Huntington Beach Drive, Fairport Harbor, OH 44077; 440-639-9972
www.lakemetroparks.com/parks-trails/fairport-harbor-lakefront-park-2

Even your dog has a place to swim at this small beach near Fairport Lighthouse. The pet area is off to one side and allows Fido and friends to enjoy the water. The main beach has a parking area (it has a small fee) and also offers concessions, restrooms, and showers. A wheelchair-accessible boardwalk is senior-friendly and lined with benches and picnic tables. Fairport Beach is also a great place to learn a water sport. There's an extensive summer schedule of private 90-minute lessons on kayaks, paddleboards, sailboats, and personal watercraft. Equipment is available, or you can bring your own. Group lessons, known as Outreach Adventures, provide an hour of instruction and all equipment for groups of 10–30.

Headlands Dunes State Nature Preserve

9601 Headlands Road, Mentor, OH 44060; 614-265-6561
naturepreserves.ohiodnr.gov/headlandsdunes

If you want to see an Ohio beach the way the Native Americans did, come here, to one of the only preserved natural beaches in the state. The preserve is adjacent to Headlands Beach State Park, outside Mentor, and also next to the Fairport Harbor West Breakwater Light, which is privately owned and not open to the public. You can, however, get pretty close to it along a breakwater trail. The microcosm of plants and animals here begins with switchgrass and beach grass, which catch and stabilize drifting sand. The area provides a sanctuary for migrating birds and monarch butterflies. Marked trails provide safe access for visitors, and a boardwalk was being constructed in 2017. Be careful to stay on the trails to protect the fragile ecosystem.

Kelleys Island State Park Beach

920 Division Street, Kelleys Island, OH 43438; 419-746-2546
parks.ohiodnr.gov/kelleysisland

There's no lifeguard, but the water is shallow, so the beach at Kelleys Island is a good place for families to kick back and relax during their island visit. Even if you're not a swimmer, you can enjoy the water here, because the sandy shelf extends 100 feet into the lake, and you can wade to your heart's content. The island's scenic Glacial Grooves are across the road, and the state park's fishing pier, boat ramp, and walking trails are nearby. There are restrooms and changing rooms, plus kayak rentals. A number of ferry services (including car ferries) are available to take you to the island.

Maumee Bay State Park Beach

1400 State Park Road, Oregon, OH 43616; 419-836-7758
www.stateparks.com/maumee_bay.html

Beachgoers have two choices here. You can opt for the half-mile lakeside beach, or move a short distance to a 57-acre inland lake, which also has a sandy beach, plus a lifeguard. Personal watercraft

are available for rent on the Lake Erie side, as are canoes, kayaks, and paddleboats at the inland lake. An amphitheater between the beaches hosts weekend entertainment during the summer.

7 Nickel Plate Beach

Nickel Plate Drive, Huron, OH 44839; 419-433-8487
coastal.ohiodnr.gov/erie/nickelplate

Ohio's largest beach, just east of the Huron River, has a soft, natural sand beach, picnic areas, and restrooms. There's a $5 parking fee during the summer, but winter visits for beach walking and bicycling are free. Small, flat stones can be found on the beach and are popular for skipping and rock painting. The play areas include an outdoor ping-pong table and beach volleyball courts (bring your own equipment). Be sure to get a picture of the giant Adirondack chair. Visitors should remember that there is no lifeguard on duty, and potentially dangerous rip currents have been known to occur here.

8 Walnut Beach Park

Lake Avenue and Walnut Boulevard, Ashtabula, OH 44004; 440-993-7036
coastal.ohiodnr.gov/ashtabula/walnutbeachpk

Long stretches of pretty, foot-friendly beach are here, making it a great place to search for beach glass—manmade glass that has been rounded by the waves. The 28-acre park has plenty of amenities, starting with the Ashtabula Harbor Light on one side, plus a 1.4-mile breakwater for fishing. There is a wheelchair-accessible boardwalk, a nature trail, and walkways over dunes and wetlands. Courts for beach volleyball and basketball are here, along with a skate park and playground. The Great Ohio Lake-to-River Greenway has its northern terminus at the park. An annual Beach Glass Festival is held at the harbor in June, attracting collectors and artists.

Sunset on a Kelleys Island beach

Marina and Perry's Memorial, Put-in-Bay

For a Midwestern state, Ohio boasts some beautiful islands, complete with scenic vistas and nightlife with a definite island vibe. Kelleys Island is a bit of an upscale place, with pricey (but so worth it) bed and breakfast inns. South Bass Island, with the feisty tourist town of Put-in-Bay, is where that nightlife can be found. Tiny Middle Bass Island is known for its winery history and its more-modest lifestyle. North Bass has no commercial development and just a few dozen residents.

ISLAND DESTINATIONS

1 Kelleys Island

240 East Lakeshore Drive, Kelleys Island, OH 43438; 419-746-2360
www.kelleysislandchamber.com

This is one of the most popular day trips in northern Ohio. From Sandusky, Port Clinton, Catawba Island, or Lorain, hop on a ferry with your bicycle and a picnic basket, and spend the day in an island state of mind. Don't worry: if you're not a cyclist, there are plenty of golf carts for rent (be sure to ask if the battery is fully charged). The downtown area is filled with graceful Victorian homes and bed and breakfasts. The three-story Kelleys Mansion is open for tours, and it even has a widow's walk (a raised platform harking back to the days when sailing widowed many women). Near the mansion, don't miss Inscription Rock, carved with Native American symbols. Have lunch, explore the town, see the state park, and enjoy your day.

2 Middle Bass Island

Middle Bass, OH 43446; 866-644-6727
www.middlebass.org

Middle Bass was home to the Lonz, Bretz, and Rehberg wineries, and long rows of grapes once dominated the island. Today, the Lonz property has been incorporated into Middle Bass Island State Park. Surprisingly, the island boasts some Civil War history. Confederates disguised as passengers from Canada boarded the lake steamer *Philo Parsons* and sailed it to Middle Bass, where they attacked and sank the *Island Queen*. Their ultimate objective was the USS *Michigan*, but they were foiled. Returning to Canada, most of the raiders were captured and one was hanged. Besides the state park and its camp-ground, the island has several restaurants, golf cart rentals, a general store, four nature preserves, and plenty of birding opportunities.

3 North Bass Island

Isle St. George, OH 43436; 419-734-4424
parks.ohiodnr.gov/northbassisland

There is no scheduled ferry service to this island, so access is by private boat or plane. Only a few families live there, and children must go to school off-island. Firelands Winery in Sandusky leases land from the state park for a vineyard, thus maintaining the island's heritage. Otherwise, there is no commercial development. At the state park, which occupies most of the 688-acre island, primitive camping is available by special permit. Boat tie-up is free, and fishing requires only an Ohio license.

South Bass Island

Put-in-Bay, OH 43456; 419-285-2832
www.visitputinbay.com

Shaped like a lopsided barbell, South Bass has a small northern section that is mostly residential, an isthmus that is home to the 352-foot-tall Perry's Victory and International Peace Memorial, and a larger southern section that holds the tourist town of Put-in-Bay. There you can hop the Tour Train (powered by Jeep) to see the sights, but be aware that pickup service at each stop can be erratic. Be sure to visit the Peace Memorial, which commemorates the Battle of Lake Erie during the War of 1812. Commander Oliver Hazard Perry sailed from Put-in-Bay to defeat the British, and after doing so, famously reported, "We have met the enemy, and they are ours." After your tour, retire to a bar or restaurant in town to enjoy some live music, a cool drink, and the Key West–like ambience.

Marblehead Lighthouse at dawn, Marblehead

Given their purpose and history, lighthouses automatically evoke feelings of romance and adventure. You want to know their stories, how they were built, the people who served in them, and what happened to them after their era was over. You'll be happy to know that some of these lighthouses are still open to the public as museums or attractions. Even those that are closed to the public are still frequently visited and photographed.

LIGHTHOUSES

1 Ashtabula Harbor Light

Ashtabula Harbor, OH 44004
www.ashtabulalighthouse.com

This lighthouse, first constructed in 1836, is more portable than most. The first version built was connected to a pier; 50 years later a new one was built at a different pier, but when the Ashtabula River was widened, the lighthouse was left marooned in the bay. Thirty years later it was moved from its island to a barge. The present lighthouse was built in 1905. In 1916 it was moved 1,750 feet to a concrete base. In 1927, it was rammed by a steamer and moved six inches, thus ending its travels—so far. Visits to the lighthouse are sometimes available via a floating dock during special events.

2 Cedar Point Lighthouse

1 Cedar Point Drive, Sandusky, OH 44871; 419-627-2350
www.cedarpoint.com/stay/lighthouse-point

When Cedar Point amusement park bought an abandoned Coast Guard property in 1987, a derelict lighthouse was part of the deal. The first lighthouse in the area was built in 1839 and replaced in 1862. Other range lights were added later. After Cedar Point planners acquired the lighthouse, they decided to restore it and make it the centerpiece of Lighthouse Point, a camping and cabin resort within the park. The lighthouse is just for show; it's not open to the public.

3 Cleveland Lighthouses

These lighthouses are maintained by the U.S. Coast Guard and are closed to the public, but they're still popular with camera buffs and sightseers.

Cleveland East Entrance Lighthouse
Located at the east end of the long breakwater forming the Cleveland harbor.
GPS: 41° 32.585' N, 81° 39.077' W
www.lighthousefriends.com/light.asp?ID=284

Cleveland Harbor East Breakwater Light
Located at the end of the breakwater at the east side of the entrance to the Cuyahoga River. GPS: 41° 30.612' N, 81° 42.930' W
www.lighthousefriends.com/light.asp?ID=283

Cleveland Harbor Main Entrance Light
Located at the end of the breakwater on the west side of the entrance to the
Cuyahoga River. GPS: 41° 30.538' N, 81° 43.062' W
www.lighthousefriends.com/light.asp?ID=282

Conneaut West Breakwater Light

Off Limestone Drive, Conneaut, OH 44030
www.lighthousefriends.com/light.asp?ID=288

What do you do with a lighthouse when it goes out of service? This sleek, 60-foot tower was auctioned off twice after its decommissioning and is now in private hands. Located at the end of a freestanding breakwater, it is best seen from the public boat launch on Limestone Drive, but you'll need a telephoto lens to get a good photograph. It can also be seen from several points along Broad Street. The present structure was put into operation in 1934, replacing several earlier structures in different locations.

Fairport Harbor Marine Museum and Lighthouse

129 Second Street, Fairport Harbor, OH 44077; 440-354-4825
www.fairportharborlighthouse.org/museum.htm

This is probably my favorite lighthouse in Ohio, because it's open to the public and the keeper's house has a delightfully odd addition, a pilothouse from a Great Lakes vessel. Then there's the ghost cat . . . The Fairport Harbor light isn't the prettiest you've ever seen, but you can climb the 69 iron steps to enjoy the breeze and the harbor view. In the attached former keeper's house, the museum focuses not just on the lighthouse, but on the rich history on the Great Lakes. One display features a local resident who was an engineer on the *Edmund Fitzgerald*. The pilothouse from the *Frontenac* has been added to the side of the museum, so visitors can walk directly aboard part of a real lake freighter. And that ghost cat? Its name is Sentinel, and it was the pet cat of a lighthouse keeper's wife. Its mummified remains are a creepy guard for the Founders' Room.

Fairport Harbor West Breakwater Light

Fairport Harbor, OH 44060
www.fairportharborwestlighthouse.com

All lighthouse lovers dream of living in one, don't they? Four people have tried to make the dream come true since Fairport West was first auctioned off in 2005, but none have been successful yet. The current owner celebrated the lighthouse's 87th anniversary in 2012 by beginning a complete renovation of the classic four-square structure.

In the meantime, the lighthouse remains in commission, with its automated light, foghorn, and a National Weather Service weather station all in service. There's no public access to Fairport West, but it can be seen from nearby Headlands Beach State Park, and from the Fairport Harbor Marine Museum and Lighthouse.

7 Huron Lighthouse

North Main Street, Huron, OH 44839; 419-433-8487
www.us-lighthouses.com/huron-harbor-lighthouse

It's easy to identify a 1930s lighthouse at a glance by the dramatic Art Deco design. You can walk out to this picturesque tower from the town park via a concrete fishing pier and a rocky sea wall. It's also visible from nearby Nickel Plate Beach. The first lighthouse was built here in 1835, and the present one was placed in service 101 years later. The lantern room was removed in 1972 when the light was automated. Solar panels were installed to power the new light, and its beacon can be seen for 12 miles.

8 Lorain Lighthouse

Jackalope dock: 301 Lakeside Avenue, Lorain, OH 44052; 440-204-2269 (boat tour reservations)
www.lorainlighthouse.com

This lucky lighthouse has its own charitable foundation, which organizes fundraisers, applies for grants, sees to maintenance, and keeps the historic structure open for the public. The Lorain Lighthouse Foundation started out as a Save-the-Lighthouse Committee in the 1960s, and that's exactly what they did. June through September on Tuesday nights, sunset dinner cruises take passengers out from the Jackalope Lakeside Restaurant dock for a four-course meal with wine, followed by a lighthouse tour. Boat tours are also offered; check for a specific schedule. For a distant view of the lighthouse, walk the pier behind the Jackalope Lakeside Restaurant.

Marblehead Lighthouse

110 Lighthouse Drive, Marblehead, OH 43440; 419-734-4424
www.marbleheadlighthouseohio.org

Though the lighthouse and keeper's house are part of Marblehead Lighthouse State Park, the Marblehead Lighthouse Historical Society maintains the museum in the picturesque and charming keeper's house. Nearby there's a replica of the 1876 U.S. Lifesaving Station, complete with a restored Coast Guard rescue boat on a launching railway. Also, don't miss the Wolcott House, home of a former keeper, which is also open for tours 2.7 miles away at 9999 East Bayshore Road. The museums are free, but if you want to climb the lighthouse itself, there's a $3 charge. Up the 77 steps, you can see several of Lake Erie's islands and the Cleveland shoreline.

Port Clinton Lighthouse

West State Route 163, Port Clinton, OH 43452; 419-797-2504
www.portclintonlighthouse.org

It could have been a sad ending. The 26-foot Port Clinton Lighthouse, a replacement to an earlier one, was built in 1896 and saw service for some 30-odd years. It was moved from a breakwater to a marina in 1952, then later forgotten and left to deteriorate. In 2005 the owner talked to the city, and the Port Clinton Lighthouse Conservancy was formed. With a combination of grants and donations, the little structure was restored in 2014. Two years later, on an overcast August day, it was moved to Waterworks Park and raised by crane onto new concrete piers. The lighthouse is open limited hours Fridays though Sundays.

Toledo Harbor Lighthouse

Lighthouse Landing: 4441 North Summit, Toledo, OH 43611; 419-691-3788
www.toledoharborlighthouse.org

This could be the most unique lighthouse in Ohio. Four stories rise above a 20-foot crib base, making it 85 feet tall, with 4,000 square feet. It is built of buff brick with Romanesque arches and features a rolled-edge steel roof. The round metal tower at the top supports the lantern room. Completed in 1903, the lighthouse was automated in 1966 and is still lit today. Its original Fresnel lens has a new home at Quilter Lodge in Maumee Bay State Park. A renovation effort has been underway since 2003, led by the Toledo Harbor Lighthouse Preservation Society. The Society hosts regular fundraising events, and occasionally offers tours by boat. The best viewing for this lighthouse is from the water, so bring or rent a boat for an up-close look. You may see the lighthouse "ghost," which is actually a mannequin named Sarah in an upper-story window.

12 Vermilion Lighthouse

480 Main Street, Vermilion, OH 44089; 440-204-2400
www.lighthousefriends.com/light.asp?ID=280

You might call it "The Case of the Missing Lighthouse." The 34-foot tower visitors see today is a replica. The 1877 version was taken apart and moved away after storm damage in 1929. One of the brothers who first reported the storm damage, Ted Wakefield, always regretted the lighthouse's loss, and as an adult he headed the drive to build a replica on the grounds of the now-defunct Inland Seas Maritime Museum. A museum visitor eventually told a story that solved the mystery of the Missing Lighthouse. Olin W. Stevens, it turns out, once served as keeper at Vermilion. Later, on a new assignment, he was surprised to find himself keeping the same lighthouse in its new location. It had been reassembled on Lake Ontario at the St. Lawrence River and renamed the East Charity Shoal Light. The replica remains on the old museum grounds, but it is not open for tours.

Cleveland Harbor West Pierhead Lighthouse (it's entirely encased in ice)

Union Terminal, Cincinnati

There's something compelling about an authentic historic building. Maybe it's the thought of walking in the footsteps of long-passed people. Though Ohio is home to structures that date back centuries (see Great Serpent Mound, page 19), its architectural history is relatively recent. Still, there's much here to appreciate.

HISTORIC BUILDINGS AND ARCHITECTURE

German Village, Columbus

1 Cincinnati Union Terminal

Cincinnati Museum Center, 1301 Western Avenue, Cincinnati, OH 45203;
513-287-7000
www.cincymuseum.org/union-terminal

The western hemisphere's largest half dome—106 feet high and 180 feet across—soars over the entry to this 1930s-era passenger rail station. The principal architects were Alfred T. Fellheimer and Steward Wagner, with Paul Philippe Cret and Roland Wank serving as design consultants. More than 18,000 square feet of artwork originally adorned the station, including 23 Winold Reiss mosaic murals depicting timelines for the United States and for Cincinnati. Decorator Pierre Bourdelle painted ceilings with fantasy murals and constructed wall murals of carved linoleum. Two Maxfield Keck bas-relief carvings are in the rotunda. Some of the art was removed when the terminal was converted into a center for museums.

2 Cleveland Arcade

401 Euclid Avenue, Cleveland, OH 44114; 216-696-1408
www.theclevelandarcade.com

This five-story Victorian-era atrium spans the space between two taller buildings at each side. Balconies on the taller buildings overlook the atrium. A skylight stretches for 300 feet and is 100 feet high. Built in 1890, the structure was first used as a shopping mall. In recent years, there's been a revitalization. One building has been repurposed as a Hyatt Regency Hotel. Shops and restaurants have begun to populate the atrium and the other buildings again. I can recommend the Chocolate Bar for the perfect martini, the perfect white chocolate chicken salad, and the perfect hot chocolate to finish it off.

3 German Village

German Village Meeting Haus, 588 South 3rd Street, Columbus, OH 43215;
614-221-8888
www.germanvillage.com

This meticulously preserved neighborhood near downtown Columbus was developed in the mid-1800s by German immigrants. They built red brick homes and breweries and preserved their German culture and language. The area began to decline during Prohibition, and had become a slum by the 1950s. Revitalization began with the organization of the German Village Society and German Village Commission. Strict zoning keeps the village mostly residential, with a limited commercial area. Walking carefully along the humped brick sidewalks, visitors can enjoy the tiny front gardens behind wrought iron fences, and the tidy German-style homes. A favorite spot for many daytrippers is the Book Loft, which spreads through several attached buildings on 3rd Street and features themed sections that can vary from sprawling basement spaces to cramped second-floor closets and hallways. Be sure to greet the resident cat, who often hangs out on the mystery balcony.

Hale Farm and Village

2686 Oak Hill Road, Bath, OH 44210; 330-666-3711
www.wrhs.org/plan-your-visit/hale-farm/

Administered by the Western Reserve Historical Society, this living-history village preserves the story of the Western Reserve, which was ceded from Connecticut and opened for settlement in the late 1700s. Visitors are invited to participate in the immersive culture at Hale. Costumed docents guide visitors and help them learn about farming, crafts and trades, and colonial history. There are regular lectures and programs for adults; children can partake in farm chores and historic crafts and trades, and attend programs ranging from maple sugaring to following the Underground Railroad. The public is also welcome to reserve space in the village for weddings and special events.

Kirtland Temple

7809 Joseph Street, Kirtland, OH 44094; 440-256-1830
www.kirtlandtemple.org

The 1833 temple was the first to be built by the Church of Jesus Christ of Latter Day Saints. The building was constructed of local Berea Sandstone in a mix of Federal, Greek Revival, and Gothic Revival styles. Joseph Smith said several miracles, including a vision of the celestial kingdom, occurred in the temple. Visitors are offered a general one-hour tour, group tours, or special tours, including a Streets of the Saints Tour and a Cemetery Tour. For the Basement to Bell Tower Tour, the recommendations are flexibility and clothes that you're OK with getting a bit dirty. There's also a Handyman Tour, which costs $10 and is perfect for those with a sense of humor. A Spiritual Formation Center offers group and personal spiritual retreats.

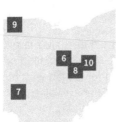

6 Malabar Farm State Park

4050 Bromfield Road, Lucas, OH 44843; 419-892-2784
www.malabarfarm.org

Pulitzer Prize–winning author Louis Bromfield built the Big House at Malabar Farm in 1940 after serving in WW I and living in France and India. Some of his novels and screenplays became movies, and he moved in Hollywood circles. On a tour of the Big House, you'll see the room where Humphrey Bogart and Lauren Bacall spent part of their honeymoon. Pugh Cabin, a day-use rental facility in the park, is part of the Shawshank Trail, since a scene from the movie *The Shawshank Redemption* was filmed there. The state park also includes a restaurant, a 19-bed hostel, and primitive camping. On the tractor-drawn farm wagon tour, you'll learn about farm techniques Bromfield used, like maple sugaring, no-till farming, strip cropping, contour farming, and grazing cells. Many locations on the tour are part of Bromfield's nonfiction work *Pleasant Valley*.

7 Paul Laurence Dunbar House

219 North Paul Laurence Dunbar Street, Dayton, OH 45402; 937-224-7061
www.nps.gov/daav/planyourvisit/paul-laurence-dunbar-house-historic-site.htm

Dunbar was one of the first African Americans to support himself entirely by writing. He was a renowned poet and author, producing a dozen books of poetry and four novels. He also wrote short stories and popular song lyrics. Admission is free, and the carefully preserved home is open Friday through Sunday. A visitor center is around the corner on Edison Street, where a film and more exhibits and artifacts are available.

8 Roscoe Village

600 North Whitewoman Street, Coshocton, OH 43812; 740-622-7644 or 800-877-1830
roscoevillage.com

This day trip will be a little slower than most, aboard the restored *Monticello III*, a horse-powered canal boat that transports visitors along part of the historic Ohio and Erie Canal at Roscoe Village, near Coshocton. The canal was a thriving concern from 1830 until the advent of railroads in 1861, and it continued to move local goods until the flood of 1913. In the late 1960s, Roscoe Village's revival began with the restoration of the 1840 tollhouse. Today, along with the authentic canal boat, visitors can take living history tours through period homes and businesses, enjoy the gardens, and see a film about the canal era. Shops and restaurants are also available. The Johnson-Humrickhouse Museum in the village has permanent exhibits on Native American and Early American history.

Sauder Village

22611 State Route 2, Archbold, OH 43502; 800-590-9755
saudervillage.org

Take a train or buggy ride to begin your exploration at Sauder, which spreads over more than 200 acres. Some 40 historic buildings are collected here, including a farm shop originally used by the founder, woodworker Erie Sauder. There's also a cabinet shop, barbershop, medical office, school, water-powered grist mill, the Elmira Train Depot, and St. Mark's Lutheran Church. Costumed docents are available in homesteads and farm buildings. Visitors can watch blacksmiths, glassblowers, bakers, spinners, and farmers work as they did in pioneer times. Special events, like apple butter weekends, rug hooking classes, a farmers' market, and Harry Potter days go on all year long. The village includes the Doughbox Bakery and the Barn Restaurant, plus a café, ice cream parlor, and coffee shop. You can even stay on the grounds, at the Sauder Heritage Inn or the Sauder Village Campground.

Schoenbrunn Village

1984 East High Avenue, New Philadelphia, OH 44663; 330-339-3636 or 800-686-6124
www.ohiohistory.org/visit/museum-and-site-locator/schoenbrunn-village
www.ohio.org/destination/new-philadelphia/educational/schoenbrunn-village

The Ohio country was still largely a wilderness in 1772, and few Europeans had visited the area. This restored village takes you back to those days, when Rev. David Zeisberger led 28 Moravians to the Tuscarawas Valley to serve as missionaries to the Delaware Indians. Their settlement lasted only five years, but another Moravian minister from nearby Dover later led an effort to salvage the village. Today, Historic Schoenbrunn consists of 16 reconstructed log buildings, a church, and the original cemetery. Costumed docents tell the story of a unique blending of German and American Indian cultures. The visitor center offers an introductory film. *Trumpet in the Land*, a nearby outdoor drama (page 34), tells the story of Zeisberger's mission.

11 Stan Hywet Hall & Gardens

714 North Portage Path, Akron, OH 44303; 330-836-5533
www.stanhywet.org

This lovely estate was the home of the Seiberling family, founders of the Goodyear Tire and Rubber Company. It was completed in 1915 and named *Stan Hywet*, Old English for "stone quarry." The 68-room Tudor Revival house is surrounded by lagoons, terraces, formal gardens, and greenhouses. It's been named the #1 house tour in America, and rightly so. You can lose yourself here. Imagine being served breakfast in the four-poster curtained bed of the master bedroom. Climb the tower to watch sunshine play across the stained glass windows. Admire the fanciful wallpaper in the nursery, or pretend the Round Room is your private hideaway. The Seiberlings always intended Stan Hywet to be a vibrant part of its community, so today the estate and its gardens are popular destinations.

12 Thomas A. Edison Birthplace

9 North Edison Drive, Milan, OH 44846; 419-499-2135
tomedison.org

It's fascinating to walk through the childhood home of a genius and wonder about his formative years. Did he look at candlelight and think, "There has to be a better way?" Maybe. It's fun to think about, anyway. Thomas Edison was born here in 1847, lived in the home until he was seven, then purchased it himself in 1906, surprised to find the rooms still lit by candles. After his death in 1931, Edison's widow and daughter decided to use the house as a memorial to his remarkable life. It was opened as a museum on the centennial of his birth. His descendents still serve on the board of trustees, with a great-great-great-nephew as president. Exhibits include family mementoes and documents, plus examples of some of his early inventions.

3 Zoar Village

Zoar Store & Visitor's Center, 198 Main Street, Zoar, OH 44697; 330-874-3011 or 800-262-6195
historiczoarvillage.com

German Separatists founded Zoar more than 200 years ago, in 1817. They considered it a utopia—a "sanctuary from evil." For more than 80 years, it was a thriving communal settlement. The religious community disbanded after the death of its founder, Joseph Bimeler, and the property was divided among the remaining residents. Today, the Zoar Community Association and the Ohio History Connection maintain a dozen of the historic homes as living-history museums. A formal three-acre flower garden in Zoar is based on the Book of Revelation and includes a central Tree of Life representing Christ. Holiday and seasonal events, including a spring Maifest, are held each year, and there are school programs, classes, and lectures. Visitors can tour the museums and gardens, stroll through the village, learn to weave a rug, or forge a nail. History talks are held on the first Saturday of each month.

Historic Buildings and Architecture

Point of Beginning monument, East Liverpool

You might say modern Ohio history started here in 1785. The survey point, established by Thomas Hutchins, opened the Northwest Territory. European settlers flocked to the Ohio country to trade with, live among, and eventually fight against local Indian tribes. This history is filled with tragedy, but also with exciting and notable achievements.

OHIO HISTORY

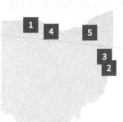

1 Fort Meigs

29100 West River Road, Perrysburg, OH 43551; 419-874-4121
www.fortmeigs.org

Taking a simple hour-long tour of this U.S. War of 1812 fort won't be enough for the curious and imaginative. Fort Meigs offers a mind-boggling array of demonstrations, lectures, themed reenactments, workshops, hands-on crafts, holiday events, and just plain fun, for everyone from toddlers to grandpas and grandmas.

The reenactments include the First Siege on Memorial Day weekend, Muster on the Maumee over Father's Day weekend, the Independence Day reenactment in July, and the Garrison Ghost Walk on two weekends in October. The British and their allies attempted to storm the fort twice but were defeated both times. The visitor center is open Wednesday through Sunday year-round, but the fort itself is only open April through October.

2 Historic Fort Steuben

120 South Third Street, Steubenville, OH 43952; 740-283-1787
www.oldfortsteuben.com

A nicely reconstructed 1786 fort along the Ohio River offers visitors a unique look at early European settlers and their lives. Named for Baron von Steuben of Revolutionary War fame, the fort was founded by the First American Regiment to protect surveyors as the Northwest Territory was being developed. The original Federal Land Office for the area is also on the site. An exhibit hall features rotating exhibits about Native Americans, Colonial life, and Ohio and American history. Archaeological digs have been conducted by the Franciscan University of Steubenville at the fort since 1978, and there is an annual summer field school for students. Other yearly activities include Frontier Days and Constitution Week. The visitor center devotes a small section to Steubenville's most famous son, entertainer Dean Martin.

John H. Morgan Surrender Site

State Route 518, 0.2 mile east of County Road 784, between Gavers and West Point, OH

It's easy to miss, and you might have to turn around a time or two, but history buffs often search out this good-size boulder along Route 518 just to read the brass plaque commemorating the surrender site of wayward Confederate Brigadier General John Hunt Morgan. Morgan wanted to draw Union forces away from the battlefields, and for two months he succeeded, as he and more than 2,000 men crossed southern Ohio, ransacking as they went. He was down to 475 men by mid-July, harassed and chased by Union troops. He made it to Columbiana County by late July, then was caught by Union troops and surrendered with 355 men. Besides the monument, a piece of the trunk of the tree under which he surrendered was saved for posterity and can be seen at Beaver Creek State Park in Lisbon.

Johnson's Island Civil War Military Prison

3510 Confederate Drive, Johnson's Island, OH 43440; 419-448-2327
www.johnsons-island.org

Many of the 206 grave markers in this National Historic Landmark bear the same word: *unknown*. The United Daughters of the Confederacy erected the markers in the early 1900s, but identifying remains has been difficult. The graves were originally topped only with wooden crosses, and records from the time are sketchy. The federal government leased half the island from the Johnson family in 1861, and more than 10,000 Confederate officers, soldiers, and a few civilians were interned here during the Civil War. The complex covered 16 acres and held more than three dozen buildings. There were many escape attempts, especially when the lake was frozen, but only a few were successful. Heidelberg University has conducted archaeological digs on the island since 1989, and the Friends and Descendants of Johnson's Island Civil War Prison (FDJI) focus on preservation, education, and research efforts.

May 4 Memorial and Visitors Center

1125 Risman Drive, Kent, OH 44243; 330-672-3456
www.library.kent.edu/special-collections-and-archives/may-4-memorial-kent-state-university

101 Taylor Hall, 300 Midway Drive, Kent, OH, 44242; 330-672-4660
www.kent.edu/may4

There's not one good thing about visiting this memorial, but it almost seems a requirement. We need to remember what happened, even if we'll never fully understand why. On May 4, 1970, four students—two of whom were just on their way to class—were killed and nine wounded

by National Guardsmen sent to quell student protests over U.S. incursion into Cambodia during the Vietnam War. The memorial is a 2.5-acre wooded, flower-decked retreat for quiet reflection. The May 4 Visitors Center is located in Taylor Hall, near the site of the shootings. It follows the university's academic calendar, so it's closed during school breaks. Escorted walking tours are offered there, along with a documentary film. A commemorative event is held every May 4.

6 McCook House Civil War Museum

15 South Lisbon Street, Carrollton, OH 44615; 330-627-3345 or 800-600-7172
carrollcountyhistoricalsociety.com/McCook/House/house.htm

The McCook homestead is a wonderfully imposing red brick example of Federal architecture at the center of Carrollton. Daniel McCook, patriarch of the Fighting McCooks, enlisted in the Civil War at age 63. Eight sons and several nephews also enlisted. Daniel, while a major stationed at Cincinnati, was sent to capture Confederate General John Hunt Morgan during his invasion of Ohio, but was killed by Morgan's troops near Buffington Island. His sons Robert, Daniel, and Charles were also killed during the war, and Latimer, a battlefield surgeon, died in 1869 of disabilities resulting from the war. The McCook House has several authentically decorated rooms, and a nice display of Civil War memorabilia. The house comes alive in November and December, with candlelight tours and a Festival of Trees.

7 Ohio History Center

800 East 17th Avenue, Columbus, OH 43211; 614-297-2300 or 800-686-6124
www.ohiohistory.org/visit/ohio-history-center

Immerse yourself in Ohio history here. Interactive exhibits start with the state's ancient beginnings and continue through westward expansion, war stories, battle flags, natural history and climate, endangered species, and the modern era. You can even learn about the Ohio-born White Castle hamburger chain. In short, the Ohio History Connection touches on nearly everything pertaining to Ohio. The museum is just the beginning, though. A genealogy research library is available here, as are resources for preserving historic homes and communities. Programs for teachers and students are offered. The campus is also home to Ohio Village.

Ohio Village

800 East 17th Avenue, Columbus, OH 43211; 614-297-2300 or 800-686-6124
www.ohiohistory.org/visit/ohio-village

This living-history museum in Columbus, part of the Ohio History Center, details the mid- to late-1800s in Ohio. There are 22 buildings, including some historic structures that were moved to the park. You won't be limited to looking at displays, though. Visitors are welcome to play with the toys, help with household chores, ride an adult tricycle around town, or browse period magazines. Town Hall, the Masonic Lodge, the Tinsmith Shop, the Ladies' Soldiers Aid Society, the Ohio Village Bank, and the Elk's Head Tavern are all places you can visit. The village's annual Halloween celebration includes a production of *The Legend of Sleepy Hollow.* The Ohio Cup Vintage Baseball Festival is also a popular annual event at the village, featuring the Ohio Village Muffins and the Lady Diamonds.

Point of Beginning

State Route 39 at the Pennsylvania line, East Liverpool, OH 43920
www.eastliverpoolhistoricalsociety.org/pob-7ranges.htm
www.youtube.com/watch?v=VxAdT2OKXy0
www.nps.gov/parkhistory/online_books/founders/sitec34.htm

A roadside obelisk in East Liverpool commemorates the beginning point of the U.S. Public Land Survey. The actual point is 1,112 feet to the south and now under the Ohio River. U.S. geographer Thomas Hutchins drove a stake there September 30, 1785, along the north-south Ellicott's Line, and used this point as the start of the east-west Geographer's Line. That stake marked the beginning of the rectangular land survey system, and its initial surveyed tract, the 42-mile-wide Survey of the Seven Ranges. Surveying therefore laid the groundwork for the wider settlement of Ohio by Europeans.

St. Helena Heritage Park

123 Tuscarawas Street Northwest, Canal Fulton, OH 44614; 330-854-6835
www.ohioanderiecanalway.com/Main/WhatsInTheArea/293.aspx

Part of the Ohio and Erie Canalway, this park covers 110 miles of the historic canal. It's an especially popular stop because of the *St. Helena III*, a canal boat replica you can ride. Horses pull the boat from a towpath alongside a section of the original canal. It's a leisurely and enjoyable way to spend an hour, riding gently along as a historian provides stories of the canal era and the surrounding countryside. Tours depart from the Canalway Center and the boat can also be chartered. The Canalway Center offers interpretive information about the area and a 30-minute introductory video.

11 Sandy and Beaver Canal

Beaver Creek State Park, 12021 Echo Dell Road, East Liverpool, OH 43920;
330-385-3091
parks.ohiodnr.gov/beavercreek
sandybeaverassoc.org

This freight canal ran 73 miles between the Ohio and Erie Canal in
Bolivar and the Ohio River at Glasgow, Pennsylvania, and included
90 locks. It was relatively short-lived, only in use from 1848 to
1852. A devastating flood, combined with the advent of convenient
railways, led to the canal system's demise. Sections of the canal still
exist, most notably alongside US Highway 30 in Hanoverton, and
at Beaver Creek State Park, where Lock 36, "Gretchen's Lock," has
been restored at Pioneer Village. Other unrestored locks are at the
park and on private property around the area. Gaston's Mill, the only
water-powered mill still working in Ohio, is also in Pioneer Village.

12 Wright Cycle Company Complex

22 South Williams Street, Dayton, OH 45402; 937-225-7705
www.nps.gov/daav/learn/historyculture/wright-cycle-company-complex.htm

The complex is part of Dayton's Aviation Trail and includes the
Wright Cycle Company building, the Wright-Dunbar Interpretive Center, and the Aviation Trail Visitor Center and Museum, which includes
the Parachute Museum. From 1895 to 1897, the Wright Brothers
operated a bicycle business here, using their profits to experiment
with powered human flight. The Interpretive Center, in the restored
Hoover Block, was originally the home of Wright and Wright Job
Printers. There they printed note cards, circulars, and newspapers,
including one published by a former classmate, Paul Laurence Dunbar, for Dayton's African American community. The Aviation Trail
also includes the brothers' burial sites, a flyable Wright B Flyer replica, Waco Airfield, the Wright Brothers Memorial at Wright-Patterson
Air Force Base, and Huffman Prairie Flying Field, where the brothers
experimented and operated a flying school.

Fort Meigs, Perrysburg

Big Muskie Bucket, Caldwell

If you're interested in geology and fossils, or think you might be, these day trips will be sure to make your bucket list. From glittering calcium carbonate to the more-humble coal and flint, Ohio has a lot to show visitors.

ROCKS AND MINERALS

1 Crystal Cave

978 Catawba Avenue, Put-In-Bay, OH 43456; 419-285-2811
www.heinemanswinery.com/crystalcave.asp

Gustav Heineman was just trying to dig a well for his winery in 1887, but instead he found the world's largest celestine geode. It was a small limestone cave to begin with, lined with a bluish mineral called celestine, a form of strontium sulfate. Originally, Heineman allowed mining of the celestite, which was used to make fireworks. That made the cave much bigger, and it turned out to be a good thing for Heineman. Just in time for Prohibition, when he had to stop making wine, he discovered that allowing tourists into the cave was a great way to make money. Tours are still a good source of revenue at the winery and are offered May through September.

2 Flint Ridge Ancient Quarries & Nature Preserve

15300 Flint Ridge Road, Glenford, OH 43739; 740-763-4127
www.flintridgeohio.org
www.ohiohistorycentral.org/w/Flint_Ridge

What has been called the "Great Indian Quarry of Ohio" doesn't look all that impressive when you drive in, but when you consider the site's overwhelming importance in the daily lives of Ohio's first human inhabitants, you start to develop a little respect. Flint Ridge has almost 8 miles of high-quality flint, 2 to 10 feet thick, in a dizzying array of colors. Besides plain old gray and white, there's pink, yellow, blue, green, black, and copper-colored flint as well. People of the Hopewell culture excavated hundreds of quarry pits to mine flint that they knapped (worked) into tools and weapons. Flint made it easy for them to hunt, butcher meat, harvest plants, make clothing, construct shelters, and defend themselves. The preserve includes a museum filled with Native American artifacts and natural curiosities, like trilobites. There are several walking trails that skirt the quarry pits, which are now filled with water.

History of Coal Museum

200 East Market Street, Cadiz, OH 43907; 740-942-2623
www.thecoalmuseum.com

Underground and surface coal mining have a long and sometimes brutal history in Ohio. A history of the industry is chronicled at this museum in the lower level of the Puskarich Public Library. Displays include tools and equipment, watch fobs, company store scrip (currency), lunch buckets, and clothing. Safety equipment on display ranges from a canary cage to self-contained rescue kits. There are coal cars, pieces of equipment, and a model of a surface mine operation. Many photographs are available, some showing smiling miners in clean clothes, and others showing exhausted, beaten-down workers after an underground shift. One chilling part of the collection is the archive of stories dedicated to mining disasters. Newspaper accounts of nineteenth-century incidents spare no details. One account reports, "The man who caused the explosion was badly mutilated. His body was burned to a crisp."

Karl E. Limper Geology Museum

Miami University, 126 Shideler Hall, Oxford, OH 45056; 513-529-3220
www.miamioh.edu/cas/academics/centers/limper-museum/

You might not think rocks and minerals are that exciting, but the glittering displays in this museum are fascinating. It houses specimens of rocks, minerals, and fossils from around the world, not to mention meteorites to boot. The museum is meant to educate students and interested visitors on basic geology, especially that of the local area. Groups of 30 or less are welcome with advance notice. Groups of more than 30 can split and rotate among the geology museum, an herbarium, and a natural history museum on the campus.

Miners' Memorial Park

State Route 78 East, McConnelsville, OH 43756; 740-962-1205
www.noblecountyohio.com/muskie.html

The centerpiece of this small picnic area in Ohio Power ReCreation Land is the Big Muskie Bucket. How big is it? Almost big enough for a two-car garage. The bucket is all that's left of the Big Muskie dragline excavator, which strip-mined coal in southeast Ohio between 1969 and 1991. Big Muskie was the largest single-bucket dragline ever built and cost $25 million in 1969. The park also includes information on the history of the Central Ohio Coal Company, and a Wall of Honor listing the company's employees.

Rocks and Minerals

6 Oakes Quarry Park

1267 East Xenia Drive, Fairborn, OH 45324; 937-754-3090
www.beavercreekwetlands.org/maplocations-oakes.html
drydredgers.org/oakes_quarry.htm

Limestone was surface-quarried here in the 1920s, and the quarry
was privately owned until the Oakes family donated it to Fairborn
in 2003. Trails through the park for hikers and horseback riders lead
through deposits of limestone fossils left by mining activity. The
Silurian Age crinoid fossils are said to be the best in the United
States. Personal collecting is only allowed from a designated pile,
which is marked by a sign.

7 Ohio Caverns

2210 East State Route 245, West Liberty, OH 43357; 937-465-4017
www.ohiocaverns.com

This is a fracture cave, which means that in some places, especially on the Historic Tour, you'll wiggle and twist and hoist yourself
through tight passageways and steep climbs. The Limestone Tour,
though, is wheelchair accessible. For those able, I recommend
combining the Historic Tour with the Natural Wonder Tour. There is
also a Winter Tour, which is all that is offered October through April.
The caverns are home to some rare and ethereal dual formations, as
well as soda straws, cave bacon, and the largest stalactite in Ohio.
The caverns are set in a pretty 35-acre park that has two pavilions
for rent, a picnic area, playground, restrooms, gift shop, and a gem-
mining sluice. Bags of mining materials can be purchased in the gift
shop, and other supplies are provided.

8 Rockbridge State Nature Preserve

11475 Dalton Road, Rockbridge, OH 43149; 614-265-6561
naturepreserves.ohiodnr.gov/rockbridge

Home a 100-foot natural bridge, this preserve is pretty basic, with
no restrooms and no pets allowed. From the parking lot, it's a bit
of a hike to the bridge, some of it alongside a steep drop-off. The
main trail is 1.75 miles. A shorter 1-mile trail in the preserve leads to
smaller rock formations. Getting to see the 100-foot natural bridge is

worth the hike, though, as long as you have some good insect repellent. It was originally the ceiling of that recess cave next door, but most of it collapsed at some point, leaving the bridge. It's possible to walk (carefully!) across the top of the bridge.

Rock House

Hocking Hills State Park, 19852 State Route 664, Logan, OH 43138; 740-385-6842
www.hockinghills.com/rock_house.html
www.oldmanscavechalets.com/hocking-hills/the-history-of-rock-house/

This is not your ordinary state park hike. Hocking Hills visitors love to follow the trail out to Rock House, a wide 200-foot-long corridor carved from rock, halfway up a 150-foot sandstone cliff. But don't worry: you don't have to climb the cliff. There's a footbridge. The trail is rugged and includes some steps. Natural columns support the roof, and there are windows and niches along the sides. From the west side of the cave, you can look through a natural window to a waterfall. Native Americans used Rock House for shelter, and as did some later unsavory types that earned the location the nickname Robbers' Roost.

Trammel Fossil Park

Tramway Drive, Sharonville, OH 45241; 513-563-1144
www.sharonville.org/188/Trammel-Fossil-Park
drydredgers.org/fieldtrips/trammel_fossil_park.htm

The Trammel family donated 10 acres for this park after rare edrioasteroid fossils—echinoderms that are relatives of sea stars, sea urchins, and other marine animals—were found there. A pavilion at the park is built in the shape of the edrioasteroid. What makes the area such a great place for fossils is the layer of upper Ordovician limestone and shale. Helpful signage around the park explains the different formations and likely fossils to be found there. Visitors are welcome to dig for fossils and keep any that they find. If you go, wear shoes that are good for climbing, and don't forget your sunscreen.

Amish buggy, Holmes County

There's plenty of fun to be had in Ohio. Do you like roller coasters? We've got that covered. Are you a cat lover? You'll be thrilled to explore the Eat, Purr, Love Cat Café. Does your idea of a day trip mean a visit to Amish country for shopping and great food? Just head to southern Ohio. Are you a fan of merry-go-rounds? Visit the Richland Carrousel Park in Mansfield and choose your ride. Whatever tickles your fancy, you'll find a trip that fits.

FUN GETAWAYS

Jaguar photographed at Akron Zoo

3 various locations in Ohio

1 Air1Airboats

2312 River Avenue, Sandusky, OH 44870; 419-366-8472
air1airboats.com

Lake Erie is fun on a ski boat, a pontoon, even a ferry, but how much more fun could it be on an airboat that skims across the water at 50 mph? The answer is a lot. It's a whole different feeling to slide over the water at high speeds on the flat-bottomed boat, turning on the proverbial dime. The airboat can navigate shallow water into secluded coves, where you might see an eagle, an egret, or a curious deer. The 40-minute daylight cruises are available from mid-May through Labor Day Weekend, and can take up to 6 people for a sightseeing tour of Sandusky Bay and the Cedar Point waterfront. During the winter, airboat ice fishing charters are popular.

2 Akron Zoo

505 Euclid Avenue, Akron, OH 44307; 330-375-2550
www.akronzoo.org

The big news at Akron Zoo for 2017 was its certification as a sensory inclusive zoo, the first in Ohio. People on the autism spectrum and others with sensory needs can be assured of acceptance and inclusion here; special access is scheduled periodically during quiet times at the zoo. Weighted blankets are available when needed, and sensory bags can be distributed with noise-cancelling headphones and other accessories. Special events at the zoo include wine tastings, senior days, holiday events, and a summer safari. There's a carousel at the zoo that features wild animals, and a solar-powered excursion train. There are also live animal shows, feeding pens, and behind-the-scenes tours. The zoo has a summer season, from April through October, and a winter season.

3 Amish Country

Holmes County Chamber of Commerce & Tourism Bureau, 6 West Jackson Street, Millersburg, OH 44654; 330-674-3975
www.visitamishcountry.com

It might be a yearning for a simpler time, or it might be that we admire them for their refusal to embrace modern technology, but whatever the reason, Amish people and their lifestyle fascinate us. Ohioans have plenty of opportunity to be fascinated, especially in the southeast, where Amish and Mennonite farms and businesses spread over five counties. The best spot in Amish country, many people believe, is Lehman's Hardware Store in Dalton. If you're in the market for a natural peanut butter stirrer, a mill to grind your own flour, or blueprints for building a windmill, this is the place to look. But don't stop there. Elsewhere in Amish country, attend a play, tour a farm, or browse through a quilt shop or a store filled with handmade furniture. Buy some cheese, try some baked goods, and, by all means, sit down at a family-style Amish restaurant.

The Carousel Works

1285 Pollock Parkway, Mansfield, OH 44905; 419-522-7558 or 800-785-8283
www.carouselworks.com

The biggest manufacturer of carousel animals in the world is open Mondays through Fridays, and tours can be arranged by phone. Each carousel, and every figure on each carousel, is handmade and custom-designed. Besides horses, more than 144 different animals, including some on the endangered species list, are offered to customers. When the company was formed in 1986, it began by restoring antique carousels and figures. Their first new construction was for Mansfield itself—the Richland Carrousel (see page 101) was completed and installed in its own park in 1991. There is still a restoration and preservation department where neglected and worn carousels and figures are brought back to life. For an insiders' look at a romantic and evocative industry, check out the Carousel Works.

Cedar Point Amusement Park

1 Cedar Point Drive, Sandusky, OH 44870; 419-627-2350
www.cedarpoint.com

For families in search of sun and fun, this is the place to go in Ohio. More than 3 million people visit the Roller Coaster Capital of the World each season. Now boasting 18 coasters, Cedar Point has been in operation since 1892, and it spreads across 364 acres on the Cedar Point Peninsula. Riding coasters is just for openers, though. At Cedar Point Beach you can chill out, ride a waverunner, or go parasailing. Take in a Wild West Revue or a Sing-Along at Planet Snoopy. More than 50 animatronic dinosaurs roar and thrash their tails, controlled from interactive consoles. You can also take a glassblowing class, dip your own candles, or be a guest train conductor. The park is open May through October.

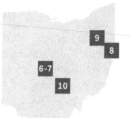

6 Columbus Zoo and Aquarium

4850 West Powell Road, Powell, OH 43065; 614-645-3400
www.columbuszoo.org

Famous in part for its director emeritus, Jack Hanna, this zoo continues to burnish its worldwide reputation. Besides the usual lions, tigers, and bears, the zoo's 7,000-plus residents include black swans, blood pythons, bonnethead sharks, golden-mantled bats, and markhor goats. One of the unique programs at the zoo is outreach, which makes animals, handlers, and speakers accessible for schools, senior citizen facilities, and events as small as a birthday party or as large as a corporate conference. Other programs at the zoo include behind-the-scenes and before/after-hours tours. Wildlife conservation tours are scheduled in worldwide destinations. The facility also includes the nearby amusement park Jungle Jack's Landing, the Zoombezi Bay Water Park, and The Wilds conservation center in Cumberland (see page 13).

7 Eat, Purr, Love Cat Café

3041 Indianola Avenue, Columbus, OH 43202; 614-852-3521
eatpurrlovecatcafe.com

It's a café that serves only drinks and bakery items prepared off-site. Reservations are recommended, and there's a $10-an-hour cover fee for adults ($5 for supervised children under 12). So what's the draw? You get to play with their cats. You can even adopt one and take it home, if you're so inclined. The café's mission is to match its customers with adult cats from the Capital Area Humane Society. A clowder of cats—that's the name for a group of felines—is always available in the cat lounge (separate from the food sales area), and the population changes daily, as the spayed/neutered and vaccinated cats are adopted. The café offers periodic special events, including Hapurry Hours, Yogatos (yoga with cats) and Purrs & Palettes (painting with cats). Check their website for their hours.

The Hall Closet

The Hall China Company, 1 Anna Avenue, East Liverpool, OH 43920; 330-385-4103
www.hlcdinnerware.com/hall_china

If you're a collector, a browser, a history buff, a fun seeker, or just a serial shopper, you'll be glad you found this small factory outlet. Hall China Company, now a subsidiary of Homer Laughlin China Company, has produced dinnerware since 1903. Their outlet, tucked into a corner of their main office building, is an irresistible stop. Go with an open mind, and you might come out with a soap dispenser, a set of ramekins, some bone china dishes, a sturdy coffee mug, or a Ronald Reagan caricature teapot that you didn't know you needed. Tours of the factory itself can be scheduled as well. The Hall Closet also carries some of HLC's Fiestaware. If you have time, make a short border jump into West Virginia to visit Homer Laughlin's outlet at 672 Fiesta Drive, Newell, WV 26050.

Hartville MarketPlace and Flea Market

1289 Edison Street Northwest, Hartville, OH 44632; 330-877-9860
www.hartvillemarketplace.com

When Sol Miller started a livestock auction in 1939, it didn't take long to add an egg auction, rent outdoor space to vendors, and put in a lunch stand. The place has been booming ever since, so much so that Sol's son moved to larger quarters in 2002. The new complex includes the MarketPlace, with more than 100 indoor shops and as many as 800 outdoor vendors; the Hartville Kitchen restaurant, bakery, and candy shop; Hartville Collectibles & Gifts; and Hartville Hardware & Lumber. Special holiday and themed events are held throughout the year, and bus tours are especially welcome. The complex is open Mondays, Thursdays, Fridays, and Saturdays.

Hocking Hills

Hocking Hills Regional Welcome Centers, 13178 State Route 664 South, Logan, OH 43138; 740-385-9706 or 800-HOCKING (462-5464); and 16197 Pike Street, Laurelville, OH 43135; 740-332-0516
www.hockinghills.com
www.explorehockinghills.com

If you've never been to the Hocking Hills, stop at a visitor center to pick up maps and information on tours of the area by vehicle, horseback, or even hot air balloon. Then take a look at the attractions. Hiking is a popular pastime in the area's state forests, parks, and preserves. There are also zipline, canopy, and climbing/rappelling tours, as well as biking, canoeing and kayaking, fishing, and golf. Indoors you can visit wineries, arts centers and galleries, museums, an opera house, and many, many unique shops. At the Hocking Hills Candleworks in

Logan, for instance, you can mix and match scents to have a personally scented soy candle made just for you. Restaurants also abound. I can recommend Sandy Sue's Silver Diner on US Highway 33 in Rockbridge for ambiance and a great breakfast. If you decide to stay awhile, check out the Maple View Tree House from Among the Trees Lodging in Logan.

11 Jungle Jim's International Markets

4450 Eastgate South Drive, Cincinnati, OH 45245; 513-674-6000
5440 Dixie Highway, Fairfield, OH 45014; 513-674-6000
www.junglejims.com/gallery

These are grocery stores, but they're amazing ones. It boggles the mind. First, the food—there's more of everything than you can imagine. Just the cheese bar will leave you gasping. There are always food sample stations, so take time to taste some seafood or fresh fruit. Don't miss my favorite spot, the coffee bar, with 50 varieties of coffee and 20 kinds of loose-leaf tea. Then there's the sightseeing. Check out a Navy fire truck and the Cereal Bowl Band, use an outhouse photo booth, look for the scarecrow, the olive bar, the humidor, and of course, Elvis. The stores offer tours, cooking classes, and Junglefest events like wine and beer festivals, barbecues, a Fall Smash, and a Big Cheese Festival.

12 Kings Island

6300 Kings Island Drive, Kings Island, OH 45034; 513-754-5700
www.visitkingsisland.com

This massive amusement park comes with more than just roller coasters and thrill rides. It also includes Soak City—a water park with activities like the Zoom Flume, the Mondo Monsoon, and the Tropical Twister. There's also Dinosaurs Alive! with controllable animatronic dinosaurs, several races, and an Ultimate Stunt Show. With a VIP ticket, you get front-of-the-line access to rides, behind-the-scenes tours, and reserved seating for shows. There are dozens of places to eat and drink, including Starbucks, Panda Express, and Skyline Chili. Adjacent to the park is Great Wolf Lodge, with its own indoor water park.

There's even a pet resort onsite.

³ The Olive Scene

100 North Main Street, Suite 145, Chagrin Falls, OH 44022; 440-247-7999
19132 Old Detroit Road, Rocky River, OH 44116; 440-895-9999
16734 Pearl Road, Strongsville, OH 44136; 440-783-1696
5512 Liberty Avenue, Vermilion, OH 44089; 440-963-0504
theolivescene.com

I visited the Vermilion store with friends who had been there before. They were enthusiastic and fearless about tasting infused oils, gourmet oils, robusto oils, and artisanal balsamic vinegars. There are also oils made from nuts and seeds. I was hesitant about the whole thing and never even mustered the courage to taste the aged vinegars. If you're a foodie, though, with an appreciation for textures and flavors that burst over your tongue, this is one day trip you have to take. The stores also sell table accessories, salts and seasonings, and gift sets. The owners of The Olive Scene make regular community appearances at festivals and farm markets. They also offer private parties that include more than 50 tastings, with hors d'oeuvres and desserts.

⁴ Richland Carrousel Park

75 North Main Street, Mansfield, OH 44902; 419-522-4223
www.richlandcarrousel.com

It's such a charming, welcome surprise to drive into Mansfield and see a full-size carrousel spinning merrily under an airy pavilion. What could be more fun? It's bargain fun at that, since rides are only $1, or six for $5. The carrousel is wheelchair accessible. There is a snack bar available, and box lunches can be arranged as well. Groups, whether large or small, are welcome for parties, and there are Friday cookouts periodically. Parts of the carrousel are antique and were restored at the nearby Carousel Works (see page 97), where all 52 figures were built. The downtown carrousel opened in 1991 and has spurred development and revitalization.

⁵ Rogers Community Auction and Flea Market

45625 Old State Route 154, Rogers, OH 44455; 330-227-3233
Alternate GPS Address: 45625 Walnut Street, Rogers, OH 44455
rogersohio.com/shop-with-us/shop-our-market/

If it's Friday, head to Rogers in northeast Ohio for "the Sale." Cars start backing up at the lone red light in Rogers before 10 a.m. Many of the vendors are already there, because they unloaded Thursday night and slept in their campers. Up to 1,600 vendors fill indoor and outdoor booths year-round to accommodate thousands of shoppers every Friday. The Sale opens around 7:30 a.m. and stays open until the last vendor leaves. Indoor sellers tend to concentrate on a single type of product, like books, meat and cheese, doughnuts (free samples!),

health and beauty items, tools, or tires. Outdoor vendors sell wild conglomerations of goods that draw you in to look, try, haggle, and buy. There are plenty of food vendors on-site, plus a full restaurant. Auctions for everything from eggs and household goods to firewood and tractors happen at varying times during the month.

16 Springfield Antique Show & Flea Market

4401 South Charleston Pike, Springfield, OH 45502; 937-325-0053
www.springfieldantiqueshow.com

Dozens of food vendors set up at the Springfield show for 9 weekends every year to feed more than 2,000 vendors and 20,000 visitors on the hunt for a vintage metal advertising sign, the perfect antique sideboard, or the quirky sundress your granddaughter will love. The event also features live music and beer and wine stands. Note: there is an admission fee to enter the grounds.

17 Toledo Zoo & Aquarium

2 Hippo Way, Toledo, OH 43609; 419-385-5721
www.toledozoo.org

Like all zoos of a certain age—this one is more than 100 years old—the Toledo Zoo has changed a lot. Where there used to be animals in cages, now there's an African Savanna complete with a Hippoquarium, a Primate Forest, and an Arctic Encounter. The zoo hasn't abandoned all its history, though. Many WPA buildings erected during the Depression are still in use, including the aquarium, built of stone and red brick, with its porthole windows. Visitors don't just come to interact with animals and marine life. Many head to the Aerial Adventure Course to walk 750 feet of aerial bridges and zipline over the Africa! exhibit. The course also includes the Quick Jump (30 feet), Flight Line (an 80-foot plunge) and a Challenge Course, with rope bridges, swinging log crossings, and horizontal climbing walls, among other obstacles.

Columbus Zoo, Columbus

Dawes Arboretum in autumn

Time and space for peaceful or prayerful contemplation are hallmarks of a public garden or arboretum. Yoga and tai chi are popular offerings, as are Japanese-style gardens. Some gardens listed here are for more-active people, and include children's activities and play spaces, or hiking/biking trails.

GARDENS, FLOWERS, AND ARBORETUMS

1 Cox Arboretum

6733 North Springboro Pike, Dayton, OH 45449; 937-275-7275
www.metroparks.org/places-to-go/cox-arboretum/

Part of the Five Rivers Metroparks system, Cox is the home of the Tree Tower, which is so pretty you can't help but climb it, not even minding the 81 steps. A viewing platform at the top provides a panoramic view of the Miami Valley and the arboretum's conifer collection. The arboretum is also the home of the Bell Children's Maze, constructed of 1,175 boxwoods, and the Butterfly House. Wear a bright yellow shirt to encourage butterfly landings. Pollinator Gardens are just outside the Butterfly House. The Conservation Corner and Zorniger Education Campus are used for education in sustainability, environmentalism, and restoration ecology.

2 Dawes Arboretum

7770 Jacksontown Road Southeast, Newark, OH 43056; 740-323-2355 or
800-44-DAWES (32937)
dawesarb.org

Nature-lovers and self-taught naturalists Beman and Bertie Dawes planted more than 50,000 trees on their 293-acre farm before they founded the arboretum in 1929. Today, visitors come in every season to explore. The Japanese Garden is an especially exquisite, serene space, with flowing water that showcases the natural landscape. It complements the Bonsai Collection in the visitor center. Don't miss Azalea Glen, the Learning Garden courtyard, and the Cypress Swamp, home to many salamanders. You'll need good shoes and a permit to hike the woodland trails at Arboretum East. The Dutch Fork Wetlands feature an observation deck, six pools, and diverse wildlife. The Italianate Daweswood House Museum is also open for tours.

Fellows Riverside Gardens

123 McKinley Avenue, Youngstown, OH 44509; 330-740-7116
www.millcreekmetroparks.org/visit/places/mill-creek-park/fellows-
riverside-gardens/

The 12-acre garden is part of the Mill Creek Metroparks in Youngstown.
Since 1963, they've featured formal rose gardens, where new varieties are tested, as well as tree collections and displays of annuals
and perennials. At the education center, a café and classrooms host
lectures on horticulture and art. A Victorian gazebo and the Kidston
Pavilion are frequently used for weddings, as well as photo backdrops.
The garden's most colorful feature is provided by 40,000 spring bulbs,
followed by seasonal displays of annuals and perennials. Garden tours
are available, and the Garden Café offers a good lunch selection. Yoga,
tai chi, kids' clubs, and family-fun programs are also on the schedule.

Holden Forests & Gardens

9550 Sperry Road, Kirtland, OH 44094; 440-946-4400
www.holdenarb.org

Seven trails wind through these gardens; the trails range from 0.75-
mile to almost 3 miles long. They provide views of Corning Lake,
conifer and beech-maple forests, and meadows filled with field-nesting
birds. Be aware that some have steep steps. There are also two rhodo-
dendron gardens and a butterfly garden. The display garden includes
a hedge collection and a lilac collection. A lotus pond and a lily pond
showcase water plants. Interesting spots to visit include the Habitat Hut
with children's activities, the 120-foot Kalberer Emergent Tower, and
the canopy walk.

Kingwood Center Gardens

50 North Trimble Road, Mansfield, OH 44906; 419-522-0211
www.kingwoodcenter.org

Formerly a private estate, Kingwood was opened to the public in 1953.
Offices and a horticultural library are housed in Kingwood Hall. The
main floor is open for self-guided tours during the week, and it still
contains original furnishings. Guided tours of the Hall are offered on
weekends. The hall is surrounded by 47 acres laid out in a variety of
themes; there are seasonal and historic gardens, those dedicated to
herbs, as well as terrace, woodland, and perennial gardens. The Allée
between the hall and Draffan Fountain is an excellent spot from which
to view spring flowers and flowering trees and shrubs. Admire the
resident peacocks as you explore the grounds. Kingwood offers workshops, children's programming, and special events, and it is a popular
wedding venue.

6 Spring Grove Cemetery and Arboretum

4521 Spring Grove Avenue, Cincinnati, OH 45232; 513-681-7526
www.springgrove.org

It's odd that an 1844 cemetery also calls itself an arboretum, but it was founded by members of the Cincinnati Men's Horticulture Society and later enhanced by a landscape architect who designed a "garden cemetery." More than 200 exotic trees were planted in the mid-1800s, though a small forest preserve in a ravine has remained untouched. In the 1920s, the flower collection was enlarged, and the arboretum continues to evolve today. The property is a National Historic Landmark and contains many State Champion trees, both native and non-native, and has had National Champion trees in the past. Notables buried there include one of the cemetery founders, several Civil War generals, Supreme Court jurist Salmon P. Chase, prominent members of the Taft family, and business leaders like Bernard Kroger, William Procter, James Gamble, and Charles L. Fleischmann.

7 Toledo Botanical Garden

5403 Elmer Drive, Toledo, OH 43615; 419-536-5566
metroparkstoledo.com/explore-your-parks/toledo-botanical-garden/

The Toledo Botanical Garden's Discovery Trail encompasses all 66 acres of the garden. Themed spaces include an herb garden, a shade garden, a vegetable garden, a rose garden, a perennial garden, and a pioneer garden. An artists' village includes buildings for potters, glassblowers, stained glass artists, and more. The Blair Museum of Lithophanes is also on the grounds. A lithophane, visitors discover, is a tiny porcelain plaque carved in three dimensions. When backlit, the bare carving is transformed into an amazingly detailed scene. The garden is also host to the annual Crosby Festival of the Arts.

Topiary Park

480 East Town Street, Columbus, OH 43215; 614-645-0197
www.topiarypark.org

Topiaries are living sculptures fashioned out of plants, and one of the fascinating things here is that you can see a topiary in the making. On some of the living yew sculptures, metal skeletons can still be seen as a ghost image of the eventual finished topiary. The garden's centerpiece is a topiary re-creation of Georges Seurat's painting, *A Sunday Afternoon on the Isle of La Grande Jatte*. The scene includes 54 human figures, 8 boats, 3 dogs, a monkey, and a cat. You have to stand in a particular spot to see it from the right viewpoint, but if you know the painting, the view is unmistakable. The 7-acre park, which was once the site of the Ohio School for the Deaf, also showcases 220 trees in 25 varieties, formal flowerbeds, and walking trails.

Wegerzyn Gardens Metropark

1301 East Siebenthaler Avenue, Dayton, OH 45414; 937-275-7275
www.metroparks.org/places-to-go/wegerzyn-gardens/

This is a good place for your kids to get dirty and wet. The Children's Discovery Garden encourages hands-on activity. Kids are encouraged to touch the plants, play in the dirt, experiment with sand art, and splash in the water. The Discovery Garden is open March through December, though the park itself is open all year. For adults, the formal Federal, English, and Victorian gardens (and the rose garden) attract home gardeners looking for design ideas and techniques. The Stillwater River Trail is the place to be for spring color and autumn leaves, and provides access to other Metroparks. The whole family can search for fairy shrimp in the vernal pools of the Swamp Forest, or hike the 1-mile Marie Aull Nature Trail. While you're there, look for the Pedestal Oak between the parking lot and gate.

Amish winery in snow

Daytrippers in Ohio expect to find wineries along the shores of Lake Erie and the Ohio River, but there are actually distinct wine regions across the state: the Appalachian region, Canal Country, Capital City region, Lake Erie Shores and Islands, and the Ohio River Valley. Ohio also boasts small artisan distilleries and nano- and microbreweries—far more than can be included in one volume.

GOOD SPIRITS
AND GOOD TIMES

An American Symbol in the Brewery District, Columbus

1 Biker Brewhouse

BikeTown Harley Davidson
5700 Interstate Boulevard, Unit B, Youngstown, OH 44515; 330-520-2266
bikerbrewhouse.net

What are you in the mood for: Pushrod Pale Ale, Kickstand Kölsch ale, or Piston Porter? The drinks here are motorcycle-inspired, and all are brewed with fresh, local ingredients. Piston Porter for instance, contains maple syrup, and a key ingredient of Kickstand Kölsch is honey. Beer is available in sampler sizes, pints, growlers, or kegs. For relaxing with a brew in biker ambiance, there's a pub table in the dealership's lounge, plus a brewhouse and balcony upstairs. A meeting room is available for private parties.

2 Cornerstone Brewing Company

58 Front Street, Berea, OH 44017; 440-239-9820
74-70 West Main Street, Madison, OH 44057; 440-983-4520
cornerstonebrewing.com

Inventive and enticing names are a staple of brewpubs, and Cornerstone is no exception. At either location, try out Angry Gorilla, a German wheat ale; Pleasurable Demise, a fruit-infused pale ale; or Summer Nights, a dark ale for a hot summer night. A full menu is available to go along with tastings. Start with brewers' pretzels, move on to beer onion soup, and complete your meal with bourbon-glazed salmon.

3 Country Porch Winery

2282 Wilson Sharpsville Road (State Route 305), Cortland, OH 44410; 330-638-0000
www.countryporchwinery.com

A very pretty front porch with rocking chairs and a small bar welcomes visitors to this winery. Using locally sourced juices, the wines here are inventive and tasty. Country Café, for instance, is made with coffee. Seyval Certain Gold contains hints of pear, apple, and lemon. Celebrate D'Vine is a crisp apple meant to be served with holiday meals. The winery offers a fresh seasonal menu filled with Ohio products—appetizers, salads, soup, sandwiches, and desserts. Sangria is available by the pitcher. Psychic Reading Night and Trivia Night are among the special events. The winery is also rentable for special events. The Country Porch is open afternoons and evenings, Wednesdays through Saturdays.

Fibonacci Brewing Co.

1445 Compton Road, Mt. Healthy, OH 45231; 513-832-1422
fibbrew.com

Yes, that's a mathematical reference in the name, but you'll have to ask them to explain it. Fibonacci's produces four foundational beers, the Tollhouse, an American stout; Earth Daisy, named for a newspaper reporter; Dummy Tripel, named for a Cincinnati Reds player; and Oberhausen, a German-inspired beer. There are also many seasonal offerings, with names like Lemon Zingibeer, Pepo Acer (described as a pumpkin porter aged with maple-bacon doughnuts), and Galacto, Brute? There's also wine on tap and bottled.

The Grape and Granary

915 Home Avenue, Akron, OH 44310; 330-633-7223 or 800-695-9870
www.renartisan.com

It started out as a simple homebrewing supply store, until the owners decided to try their hands at winemaking and distilling themselves. The Grape and Granary Winery and Renaissance Artisan Distillers are also on the premises, complete with tasting rooms and a line of products (no tastings or alcohol sales on Sunday). The winery offers a very nice Traminette, along with Blackberry Cabernet, Jalapeno Pepper Wine, and more. At the distillers, visitors can tour the operation and choose tastings from gin, single malt whiskey, grappa, rum, coffee liqueur, and (mmmmmm) limoncello.

The Hairless Hare Brewery

738 West National Road, Vandalia, OH 45377; 937-387-6476
www.hairlessharebrewery.com

Matt Harris and Mike Legg, guys with a sense of humor, founded the brewery in 2013, and they seem to be doing well for themselves. They brew on-site, aiming both for craft beer aficionados and those new to the style. They offer Crooked Hare Altbier, of course, along with a Wheels of Soul Pineapple IPA, barrel-aged Cold War Stout, Sister Cities Ale, and something called Rye the Hell Knot. They also offer a limited menu of pizza, starters, and sandwiches—perfect food to go with beer.

Maize Valley Winery and Brewery

6193 Edison Street Northeast (State Route 619), Hartville, OH 44632; 330-877-8344
www.maizevalley.com/ohio-farmers-market/

First there's the winery, where a variety of wines are made from French-American Hybrid grapes grown right on the farm's 10 acres.

The offerings include a sweet White Winter, a dry red Secret Stash, and Hanky Panky sweet white, plus many others. Then there's the brewery. Beers available all year are Hopnesia and Red Axe IPAs, Café Cubano Stout, and Vanilla Porter, among others. Along with your tastings, appetizers and desserts or casual lunches and dinners can be added. Then there's the Farm Market, where produce grown on the farm is sold. Special events are a big deal at Maize Valley, and they're family friendly. Besides the fall harvest festival, there are vintage car shows, trivia nights, vintners' dinners, and live music nights.

8 Meier's Wine Cellars

6955 Plainfield Road, Cincinnati, OH 45236; 513-891-2900
meierswinecellars.com

They're the oldest and largest wine producer in the state, thanks to grape juice. Meier's started out as a grape juice company in the late 1800s, then made wine, and then returned to their roots during Prohibition, making a sparkling Catawba juice. Today they still produce sparkling nonalcoholic grape juice, along with 45 varieties of wine. Their best-known product is #44 Cream Sherry, though I'm partial to their blackberry wine. When you visit, take advantage of the hors d'oeuvres available to complement tastings. The retail store and tasting room are open to the public, but check online for hours.

9 Merry Family Winery and Old Mill Craft Beer

2376 State Route 850, Bidwell, OH 45614; 740-245-9463
merryfamilywinery.com

A surprise offering on the wine list is Mothman Legend, a mysterious dry red. You might have to be an Ohioan to understand that, as the "Mothman" is the subject of local lore. There's also a Southern Belle Muscato and a Sweet Granny apple wine. The Blue Merry Blush is a red grape/blueberry blend that, they say, pairs well with a blueberry muffin. The cherry and cranberry wines are 100 percent fruit. Old Mill Craft Beers, made with hops grown on-site, include Hop Lizard IPA, Black Lager, pilsner, and ale. They also make their own root beer. The winery is a popular event venue, offering music, cork and canvas nights, wine and food pairing events, and private parties. Tours of the winery and vineyards are offered daily.

Northside Distilling Co.

922 Race Street, Cincinnati, OH 45202
www.northsidedistilling.com

Three distillers and a marketer make up the Northside Distilling team. They distribute to an impressive list of liquor stores, but also sell their products themselves from a downtown bar and tasting room, where you can also order from a rotating menu of cocktails made from their products, which include corn whiskey and moonshine. They welcome people who just stop by for a look and a taste, but a more formal tour of the distillery can also be scheduled. Call to check for hours.

1 Ohio Wine Association

1 South Broadway, Geneva, OH 44041; 440-466-4417 or 800-227-6972
www.ohiowines.org

Suppose you'd like to explore some of the state's wineries but have no idea how to go about it. Head to the Ohio Wine Association's website, sponsored by the Ohio Wine Producers Association. They've collected handy lists of Ohio wineries by region. Each regional list includes contact information, an address, and a brief description of each winery. The list also includes information on nearby attractions, events, lodging, and even transportation options for those who imbibe too much.

2 Old Firehouse Winery

5499 Lake Road East, Geneva-on-the-Lake, OH 44041; 440-466-9300
www.oldfirehousewinery.com

Their logo is, of course, a Dalmatian wearing a red fire helmet. Old Firehouse is a large, busy place in the resort town of Geneva-on-the-Lake, and fun-seeking daytrippers make it a priority stop. They don't even have to be wine drinkers. There's a vintage Ferris wheel at the edge of the lake, live music on summer weekends, a craft fair every summer Saturday, and regular events like a Celtic Feis (festival), a barbecue fest, a clambake, and a blues festival. Then there's the wine. The Firehouse label includes regular offerings, like Concord, Catawba, and Niagara, but there's also Apple Ice wine and Raspberry Reflections.

3 Soine Vineyards

3510 Clark Shaw Road, Powell, OH 43065; 740-362-5741
www.soinevineyards.com

Visitors are welcome to tour the winery and take advantage of the tasting room, but please note that Soine (soy-nee) isn't open every day.

14   15

Call and check for hours. Wines offered include award winners such as Fusion, Landot Noir, and Chambourcin, Cayuga White, and Traminette. Appetizers, pizza, and nonalcoholic drinks are available with tastings. Music is offered on summer weekends.

14 Staley Mill Farm and Indian Creek Distillery

7095 Staley Road, New Carlisle, OH 45344; 937-846-1443
www.staleymillfarmanddistillery.com

From the 1860s until Prohibition, the Staley family made whiskey. Production didn't begin again until 2011, when the current member of the Staley family and her husband began again with a double copper distilling method. The family takes pride in crafting what they call "frontier whiskey" in small batches with traditional methods. Aged and unaged rye whiskey and bourbon mash whiskey are sold here, along with a farm-produced maple syrup that includes a bit of rye. The farm hosts musical events, holiday open houses, living history events, and even a sip and smoke day. The distillery is open Tuesdays through Saturdays, with Sunday hours at Christmastime. There's a rustic tasting bar and retail shop, and tours of the distillery and farm are offered.

15 Watershed Distillery

1145 Chesapeake Avenue, Suite D, Columbus, OH 43212; 614-357-1936
watersheddistillery.com

With careful attention to detail and a passion for their work, the partners at Watershed craft products the old-fashioned way, with deliberate thoughtfulness. They proudly offer tours of the distillery (they last more than an hour) and then invite participants to visit their bar and restaurant, open evenings, Tuesdays through Saturdays. Besides their own bourbon, vodka, gin, and nocino, the Watershed bar offers a full slate of wines and beers, plus nonalcoholic drinks. At the restaurant, there are normal Midwestern dishes like walleye, pork chops, and burgers, but they also serve other luxury fare.

Ohio is home to many fine breweries

Carillon HIstorical Park, Dayton

Being that this is Ohio, of course, there's plenty of airplane history. There are museums and history centers all over the state. Some of them even offer rides in vintage aircraft. For railroad adventure, check out the schedules and special events at these centers of railroad history.

AIRPLANES AND RAILROADS

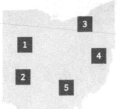

1 Armstrong Air & Space Museum

500 Apollo Drive, Wapakoneta, OH 45895; 419-738-8811
www.armstrongmuseum.org

Walking up to this small museum in Wapakoneta inspires awe in any
visitor. A 56-foot white sphere rises out of the green banks topped
by angular concrete wings, suggesting a journey to the moon. The
entrance is even more striking at night, when blue runway lights
illuminate the sidewalk, and the sphere glows. Neil Armstrong, and
other Ohioans who have taken to the air, are honored here. The
museum opened in 1972 in Armstrong's hometown. Exhibits include
the first plane that 15-year-old Armstrong flew, an Aeronca Champion, as well as Gemini and Apollo memorabilia, interactive exhibits,
and simulators. The lunar module simulator is especially exciting,
because you can feel pressure, manipulate controls, and imagine
yourself in charge of a moon landing. The Astro Theater inside
the dome offers views of the night sky and a 25-minute film of the
Apollo 11 moon landing.

2 Carillon Historical Park

1000 Carillon Boulevard, Dayton, OH 45409; 937-293-2841
www.daytonhistory.org

You could spend days wandering through this 65-acre park and still
not see everything. Focusing on transportation, though, is a good
place to start, so start off at the Wright Brothers Aviation Center.
Here you can see a 1905 *Wright Flyer III*, the first practical airplane,
which is itself a National Historic Landmark. Moving along through
the park, you can visit a replica of the Deeds barn, where inventor
Charles Kettering and colleagues invented the first electric self-start-
er for automobiles; a furnished 1894 train station originally located
in Bowling Green; a 1907 railroad watchtower from Dayton; a collection of antique bicycles; the original Miami and Erie Canal Lock #17;
and the James F. Dicke Family Transportation Center, which houses
various railcars, cabooses, and trolley cars. The park's Rail and
Steam Society operates scale trains on a limited schedule.

Cuyahoga Valley Scenic Railroad

Peninsula Depot, 1630 West Mill Street, Peninsula, OH 44264; 800-468-4070
www.cvsr.com

There's something about a steam train engine that just gets people excited. First, you hear a clanking, hissing noise as the locomotive appears. It's so massive that it dwarfs the station and the crowd. Steam billows out from beneath, and the wheels squall as the train slows to a stop. All aboard! Even if all you do is ride from one end of the Cuyahoga Valley to the other and back again, a trip aboard the Cuyahoga Valley Scenic Railroad is something to remember. Dozens of bicyclists, hikers, and kayakers are at every stop with another agenda, though. They hop on and off at stations along the way, get some exercise, then hop back on to return to their vehicles. An added attraction is the option to travel in luxury aboard the Paul Revere Car, a restored parlor car built in 1951 for Pennsylvania Railroad's Senator and Congressional east coast fleets. The CVSR also hosts special events, like evening excursions, brew nights, a murder mystery trip, and canvas and wine events.

Dennison Railroad Depot Museum

400 Center Street, Dennison, OH 44621; 740-922-6776
dennisondepot.org

Built in 1873, this National Historic Landmark is famous for its ties to World War II. Doing what they could to support the war effort, volunteers met servicemen at railroad stations all around the country, offering food, coffee, and moral support at free canteens. The 1.3 million people entertained h ìre nicknamed this depot Dreamville, USA. The museum includes railroad exhibits, a gift shop, and a restaurant. On display are two steam locomotives, freight and passenger cars, and a military hospital car. A Pullman Sleeper is being restored as a bed and breakfast car. There is a Bing Scavenger Hunt for kids, an interactive railroad car, and a model train room. Oh, and visitors can still get free coffee and a cookie in the museum lobby.

Hocking Valley Scenic Railway

33 West Canal Street, Nelsonville, OH 45764; 740-753-9531
www.hvsry.org

Operating on weekends and holidays, the railway offers countryside tours with a 1952 diesel locomotive, and passenger cars built in 1927 as commuter cars for Chicago. Some are easygoing scenic tours that include historic sights like Hocking Canal Lock #19 and the historic buildings of Haydenville, a company town for a brick and clay company. Others are holiday events like the popular Easter Bunny train (with an

egg hunt) and the New Year's Eve special, which includes either pop and pizza or wine and cheese and finishes off with fireworks. Every summer, several train "robberies" are staged. In October, extra trains travel on Fridays to take advantage of fall foliage. And of course, the Santa Train has run every December for the past 30 years.

6 International Women's Air & Space Museum

Burke Lakefront Airport, 1501 North Marginal Road, Suite 165, Cleveland, OH 44114; 216-623-1111
iwasm.org/wp-blog/

Women have been part of air and space exploration since 1804, when Napoleon Bonaparte named Madame Blanchard, a famous balloonist, as chief air minister of ballooning. In the early 1900s, Katharine Wright assisted her famous brothers in making powered flight a practical reality. In World War II, Women's Air Force Service Pilots (WASPs) tested aircraft, flew transports, and towed targets. In 1961, 13 women were chosen as the first female astronaut trainees. These and other pioneers are remembered at this small, free museum. The IWASM also offers traveling exhibits to schools and libraries.

7 Lebanon Mason Monroe Railroad

127 South Mechanic Street, Lebanon, OH 45036; 513-933-8022
www.lebanonrr.com

On most weekends of the year, and some weekdays, you can board a train here for a scenic country ride or a special event. The Turtle Creek Valley Flyer offers special group rates for schools and senior centers. Characters like Thomas the Train, Whyatt, Daniel Tiger, and Curious George travel on such children's excursions. There's a Princess Express featuring free tiaras and magic wands, and a fairy balloon artist. Adult train lovers can celebrate National Train Day, board a Wine and Beer Tasting train, or a Murder Mystery Train. In the wintertime, there's the Kinderveldt Polar Express Train, benefitting Cincinnati Children's Hospital Medical Center, and the holiday-themed North Pole Express.

Liberty Aviation Museum

Erie-Ottawa County Regional Airport, 3515 East State Road, Port Clinton, OH 43452; 419-732-0234
www.libertyaviationmuseum.org

This is a busy place, with more going on than aircraft displays. The museum's vintage planes come and go periodically to air shows and special events. Restoration is a key part of the museum's work, and visitors are welcome to observe. Georgie's Gal, a B-25J Mitchell Bomber from World War II, was restored there in 2011–12. A 1929 Ford Trimotor, which flew the Lake Erie island route for 50 years, is presently being restored. They've also acquired the PT-728 Thomcat, a World War II–era Vosper PT boat, which is currently undergoing restoration. Besides planes and the patrol torpedo boat, there's an eclectic collection of antique cars, motorcycles, and military vehicles. One of the very cool things at this museum is the Tin Goose Diner, a gorgeous '50s-style restaurant. You might have to wait for seating, but the food and ambiance are great. Special events at the museum include model plane shows, car shows, Scout Jamborees, and more.

MAPS Air Museum

2260 International Parkway, North Canton, OH 44720; 330-896-6332
mapsairmuseum.org

Even people like me who don't know much about military aircraft have heard the name Sopwith, the triplane famously flown by Snoopy in his dogfights with the Red Baron. A Sopwith Triplane replica, complete with rotary engine and wooden propeller, is on display at MAPS. The museum is also home to original fighters and bombers like a Grumman F-14B Tomcat, a McDonnell F-101F Voodoo, and a Republic F-105 Thunderchief. The museum houses helicopters, observation and training aircraft, flight simulators, and ordnance. MAPS recently acquired the collection of the former Ohio Military Museum, housing it on the second floor of the main hanger in the Ohio Military Museum Room. Regular events like Scout days, fundraisers, car shows, and holiday activities are also on the museum schedule.

National Museum of the U.S. Air Force

1100 Spaatz Street, Dayton, OH 45431; 937-255-3286
www.nationalmuseum.af.mil

Free admission and parking are great reasons to visit the vast museum at Wright-Patterson Air Force Base, but the best reason is to see the extensive collections of military flight history. Planes at the museum range from Eisenhower's Air Force One to a Lockheed AC-130A Spectre. Permanent exhibits cover the Wright Brothers, Civil War balooning, the Doolittle Raiders, and the Tuskegee Airmen. In the Early Years Gallery, you can learn the story of the 1st Aero Squadron, which placed the first tactical air unit in the field when it joined Black Jack Pershing in Texas in 1916 to make reconnaissance flights into Mexico in the search for Pancho Villa. Besides maintaining extensive indoor and outdoor exhibits, the museum has active restoration and research divisions and offers programs for adults, teachers, students, and groups.

11 Ohio Railway Museum

990 Proprietors Road, Worthington, OH 43085; 614-885-7345
www.ohiorailwaymuseum.org

Open only on Sunday afternoons, this museum nevertheless offers a lot of value for daytrippers. Since they own 2 miles of railroad right-of-way, the museum is able to offer visitors multiple rides on cars in their collection. On the railbed of the Columbus, Delaware, and Marion railway in Worthington, this museum collects locomotives, rail cars, streetcars, and interurban cars. One of their showpieces is the last CD&M interurban parlor car, the Red Bird. Their locomotive collection includes steam, electric, and diesel equipment. At the depot, collections of railroading culture and technology are on display.

PLEASE
STAY TO
THE RIGHT
→

PLEASE
STAY OFF
THE RAMP

PLEASE
STAY OFF
THE RAMP

Douglas C-124C Globemaster II at the U.S. Air Force Museum

127

The *William G. Mather*, a museum ship at the Great Lakes Science Center

Innovation, invention, science, math, ecology, botany, zoology, and geology are just some of the topics covered in the displays and programs at these museums and centers. Age doesn't matter; everyone can enjoy a day strolling through a nature center or getting serious about science at a museum.

SCIENCE MUSEUMS AND NATURE CENTERS

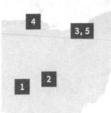

1 Boonshoft Museum of Discovery

2600 DeWeese Parkway, Dayton, OH 45414; 937-275-7431
www.boonshoftmuseum.org

Committed to hands-on science and zoology, the Boonshoft makes it easy for visitors to learn to appreciate everything from common subjects, such as our water supply, to more exotic subjects, such as meerkats and other wildlife. A treehouse that extends beyond the walls of the museum provides opportunities to learn about environmental preservation. Investigate ocean life at the Tidal Pool or nighttime desert animals at the Sonoran Desert exhibit. At Science Central, children can climb the tower and zoom down a slide, then conduct experiments in the Do Lab, or use rubber band art to learn about geometry in the Manipulative Area. There are also Discovery Camps and Scout programs offered at the museum.

2 COSI (Center of Science and Industry)

333 West Broad Street, Columbus, OH 43215; 614-228-2674
cosi.org

Since 1964, COSI has been the Ohio mecca for families and student groups. Even very young children have a great time there. At little kidspace, toddlers can climb, slide, build, and splash while they pretend to be fish, farmers, or engineers. Older children can attend a superhero breakfast, a birthday party, or a weeklong camp built around STEM (science, technology, engineering, and math) concepts. At COSI Academy, teens can explore potential careers and attend lectures and hands-on activities. For adults, COSI After Dark provides puzzles, brainteasers, and mazes, along with bar trivia contests. COSI also boasts a National Geographic Giant Screen Theater with 3D technology and 4K projection. Its 60-foot planetarium offers live shows as well as several programs.

Great Lakes Science Center

601 Erieside Avenue, Cleveland, OH 44114; 216-694-2000
greatscience.com

Great Lakes Science Center's masterful set of guiding principles have made it a leader among science centers. They believe strongly in STEM education, critical and innovative thinking, and learning through curiosity and experimentation. To that end, the Center houses MC2 STEM High School, which encourages innovative learning for future scientists, engineers, and mathematicians. Exhibits at the Center follow the same principles, starting with the NASA Glenn Visitor Center. Interactive exhibits deal with living in space, exploration, and science and engineering principles in space. A six-story dome theater surrounds visitors with massive images and sound. The steamship *William G. Mather*, a restored Great Lakes freighter, is open for tours May through October.

Imagination Station

1 Discovery Way, Toledo, OH 43604; 419-244-2674
www.imaginationstationtoledo.org

The Learning Worlds are worth exploring at Imagination Station. Little ones can learn about shapes and colors as they crawl through the tunnels of the Baby Space. Older kids can learn about forest canopies at the Tree House, or about water movement at the Wet Lab. The Little Scientist Workshops are meant for preschoolers. Older children can ride the high-wire cycle or turn themselves into a human yo-yo. There's Grow U, for future farmers, the Energy Factory, and the Extreme Science Theater. Elsewhere kids can make their own slime, construct an Alka-Seltzer rocket, make plastic milk, or freeze their own ice cream. The Station also hosts homeschool workshops, Scout programs, summer camps, and think tanks with different themes.

Lake Erie Nature & Science Center

28728 Wolf Road, Bay Village, OH 44140; 440-871-2900
www.lensc.org

You can adopt your own native animal at this center. Choose an eastern box turtle, a Cooper's hawk, or a red fox, and receive a fact sheet and adoption certificate. Wildlife education and conservation is the focus here. Programs are available for each age group, as well as for educators. The center boasts an active rehabilitation program that takes in more than 1,000 wild animals a year, returning critters to the wild as often as possible. The newly remodeled Walter R. Schuele Planetarium at the center offers Twinkle Tots for little ones and Sky-Quest for older visitors. There are also Telescope Nights, astronomy programs, and a Space Exploration Rocket Camp. Rental space and special programs are available for groups and parties.

6 North Chagrin Nature Center

401 Buttermilk Falls Parkway, Willoughby Hills, OH 44094; 440-473-3370
clevelandmetroparks.com/parks/visit/parks/north-chagrin-reservation/north-chagrin-nature-center

This 1,700-acre wildlife sanctuary, part of the Cleveland Metroparks organization, offers a full schedule of activities for fans of the outdoors. There are regular birding programs, storytelling nights, and wildflower walks. Sunset Pond offers a prime viewing area for birds, mink, muskrats, and beaver. The deck of the Nature Center overlooks Sanctuary Marsh, which was developed in 1984. The deck is a good place to view ducks and geese. Inside the Nature Center is a play space for children, wildlife exhibits, and an auditorium. There's a bird-viewing area and aquariums for fish, reptiles, and amphibians.

A Great Horned Owl, one of the species you may encounter at Ohio's nature centers.

Short North District, Columbus

There's something about a blank brick wall that makes an artist want to decorate it, or at least advertise on it. When I was a child, a blank wall overlooking Dresden Avenue in my hometown advertised Uneeda Biscuits. These days, artists are more likely to celebrate town history and the evolution of art than biscuits.

OUTDOOR MURALS

1 Dayton Murals

Dayton, OH
www.mydaytondailynews.com/news/beautiful-wall-murals-that-decorate-the-region/kluXvyUvIJ3GTFYJjxGdrO/

There's no handy, collated brochure listing all of the Dayton murals. You have to search them out one by one. The Wesley Community Center mural on Delphos Avenue is a bright, sprawling depiction of education. At Keowee and Third is a puzzling, dreamy mural featuring a young girl being pulled along by flying yellow fish—or maybe those are really balloons. At East Third and Webster is a series of delectable Veggie Murals on 20 concrete panels, perfect for pre-lunch viewing. The Egyptian Bodyshop mural adorns, you guessed it, a body shop. At Third and Linden is a 1980 historical mural depicting a farmers' market. Also on Linden, on the side of a storage facility, street artists have decorated a long wall with different themes.

2 Short North Arts District

21 East 5th Avenue, Suite 103, Columbus, OH 43201; 614-299-8050
shortnorth.org/arts-galleries/public-art/
arttrail.shortnorth.org

Many of the permanent murals in this arts district between Ohio State University and downtown Columbus are, well, interpretive. Picture the farmer's daughter from Woods' American Gothic upside-down. Or consider the meaning of Mona Lisa on her side. Or explore the Magnolia Thunderpussy mural (named after a famous burlesque dancer and restaurateur) as you walk to the Thunderpussy record shop. The Ibiza Lot mural is a work in progress, as artists continue to contribute their interpretations to it. The district also mounts a temporary mural series every year, "Six in the Short North." Instead of being painted on the buildings, they're printed on vinyl and temporarily applied with a heat-shrinking technique.

Franklin Murals

Franklin, OH 45005; 937-746-8457
www.ohioslargestplayground.com/explore/arts-culture/walking-tours/franklin-murals/219483
storiesfromtheplayground.wordpress.com/2016/06/09/a-history-of-franklin-ohio-the-city-of-murals/

The amazing thing about the Franklin murals, painted by award-winning muralist and Ohio native Eric Henn, is their perspective. At first sight, you almost think you can go into that diner for an ice cream cone, or cross the bridge between the lions, or walk across actual grass, under the painted arches, and into the painted Victorian park. The veterans' mural on the side of VFW Post 7596, at first glance, really does look like a sculpture. The transportation mural covers everything: horses, buggies, canals, steamships, railways, biplanes, and cars.

Portsmouth Floodwall Murals

Portsmouth, OH 45662
www.portsmouthohiomurals.com
www.ohiorivertourism.org/murals.html

It took nine years for Robert Dafford and his assistant Herb Roe to paint the original set of murals here. Since then, more have been added. The nearly half mile of murals is thought to be the largest assemblage painted by a single artist. Starting at the east end, the murals are chronological, beginning with the depiction of a local Hopewell mound complex. The murals progress through history, celebrating frontier notables like Shawnee leader Tecumseh and town surveyor Henry Massie. Olympic athlete Jim Thorpe, baseball legend Branch Rickey, and actor Roy Rogers are memorialized. One section depicts the 1937 flood, which was the catalyst for the floodwall itself. Steamships, farm scenes, canals, cityscapes, industry, and scenic vistas are included. Don't expect to take it all in at once, just enjoy it one mural at a time.

Steubenville Murals

Steubenville Visitor Center, 120 South Third Street, Steubenville, OH 43952; 866-301-1787
www.visitsteubenville.com/what-to-do/steubenville-murals/

"The Ladies of the Seminary" on Market Street is possibly the most thought-provoking mural in downtown Steubenville. Staring up at it, you have to wonder: Is it a coincidence that they all have the same hairstyle? Could that woman on the upper left be asleep? Did they like going to a school for young ladies, or did they hate it? All of the 23 murals make you stop and think about the way things worked in bygone days. Everything from the High Shaft Mine to a boy's first bank deposit is memorialized, depicting everyday life in an Ohio River town. There's even a mural dedicated to favorite son Dean Martin. You can walk to all of them or drive the downtown route. The Steubenville Visitor Center can also arrange guided tours.

6 Wellsville Flood Wall Murals

Lisbon Street, Wellsville, OH 43968; 330-532-9064
www.ohio.org/destination/art-exhibitsexhibitions/wellsville-flood-wall-murals
www.waymarking.com/waymarks/WM5CVF_Village_Flood_Wall__Wellsville_Ohio

Local artist Gina Hampson is responsible for painting and maintaining the murals on Wellsville's flood wall. The wall isn't in the most picturesque location, running under a bridge along Yellow Creek, but the town's revitalization committee has made the area inviting, with lighting, a sidewalk, and landscaping. The murals fill both sides of the wall and include depictions of the city's notable buildings, its pottery heritage, and the long-vanished Indian head outcropping. Some historic events are also included, notably Abraham Lincoln's visit to Wellsville a month before his assassination.

7 Yellow Springs Murals

Keith's Alley and Xenia Avenue, Yellow Springs, OH 45387
ysnews.com/news/2012/12/blog-yellowpedia-art-murals

The murals here, which you have to seek out on your own, represent many styles, from the historical to the abstract. There's even a modern version of cave art, featuring sprinting buffalo. The bicycle mural is a compelling minimalist sketch. A newer mural is a tribute to pop star Prince.

Pioneer Mural, Steubenville

Hiking trail, Chillicothe

When the last leaf and the first snowflake have fallen, Ohioans begin to think about winter activities. There's always curling up in front of the fireplace with a good book, but more vigorous activity is good, too. You can check out the downhill skiing in northern Ohio, or the cross-country skiing through the state forests and parks. Some areas have snowmobile trails. You can go ice fishing on the lakes, and in some places you can even watch a dogsled race, weather permitting.

ENJOYING THE SNOW

1 Boston Mills/Brandywine Ski Resorts

7100 Riverview Road, Peninsula, OH 44264-0175; 800-U-SKI-241 (800-875-4214)
www.bmbw.com

These side-by-side resorts open for the winter ski season as soon as snow—natural or man-made—is available. If you've never tried skiing or snowboarding, these resorts make it easy for you to get started. You can rent any equipment you need, then sign up for a Beginner Intro lesson, private lessons, or a boot camp. Just look for the Ski School sign, and you're all set. If you don't want to go down the mountain on your feet, they've got that covered, too, at the Polar Blast tubing area at Brandywine. All you have to do is jump on a snow tube and head down the tubing lanes. There are even conveyor lifts to carry you back up the hill, and you can take a break in the lodge for hot cocoa and snacks.

2 Punderson Sled Dog Classic

Punderson State Park, 11755 Kinsman Road, Newbury Township, OH 44065;
440-564-2279
www.siberiancleveland.org/Punderson-Sled-Dog-Classic.html

Because this event takes place in Ohio, it doesn't happen every year. The Siberian Husky Club of Greater Cleveland schedules a race date plus an alternate date every winter, but sometimes there just isn't enough of a good snow base at Punderson. Still, when the event happens, it's great winter entertainment. There are dogsled races in several classes, plus a skijoring race. (In skijoring, an individual dog pulls its owner along on skis.) You'll see beautifully matched teams of purebred Siberian Huskies or Alaskan Malamutes, as well as open classes for mixed teams of eager scrappers. No matter their pedigree, the dogs are always wildly excited, howling in their traces, eager to run. On the starter's signal, the dogs leap into action, and the race is on. As long as it snows, of course.

Ice Man Guide Service

Put-in-Bay, OH 43456; 419-341-9721
www.fishingcharterslakeerie.com

If you're a die-hard fisherman who doesn't mind a little cold weather, this guide service will get you through the winter, with experienced, licensed guides and all the equipment you need for a comfortable ice fishing experience. Pickups are available in Port Clinton, or you can fly to Put-in-Bay. They can transport up to 36 people per day to heated ice shanties. Tackle is provided, and guides drill the holes and provide lunch.

Mad River Mountain

1000 Snow Valley Road, Zanesfield, OH 43360; 937-599-1015 or 800-231-7669
www.skimadriver.com

Snow tubing at Avalanche Tubing Park is popular at Mad River Mountain. Besides 10 tubing lanes, there are two conveyor belt lifts, a lodge, and an outdoor fire pit. With a mountain full of trails and four terrain parks, skiing at Mad River provides hours of fun. There are ski schools for groups and individuals, youth and women's programs, and plenty of help for first timers. College Fridays during the season feature special rates for students who present a college ID. There are also homeschool days and Scout days. On some Saturday nights, live music is available at the Loft. Wednesdays are league race nights under the lights.

Snow Trails Ski Resort

3100 Possum Run Road, Mansfield, OH 44903; 419-774-9818 or 800-OHIO-SKI
(800-644-6754)
www.snowtrails.com

Open for skiing and tubing mid-December through mid-March, weather permitting, Snow Trails has multiple downhill runs and lifts, and four terrain parks, built from scratch every winter. There are also six 1,100-foot tubing runs with conveyor lifts. The Tubing Lodge has a snack bar and outdoor fire pit. Private, semi private, group, children's, and women-only lessons are available. An adaptive ski program accommodates skiers with disabilities.

6 Cross-country Skiing, Snowshoeing, and Snowmobiling

Cleveland Metroparks

Big Met Golf Course, 4811 Valley Parkway, Fairview Park, OH 44126; 440-331-1070
For ski conditions: 216-635-3270
clevelandmetroparks.com/parks/visit/activities/event-activity-types/
cross-country-skiing

Lake Metroparks

For equipment rentals: 440-256-3810
Chapin Forest Reservation, 10381 Hobart Road, Kirtland, OH 44094; 440-256-3810

Girdled Road Reservation, 12926 Radcliffe Road, Concord Township, 44077

Penitentiary Glen Reservation, 8668 Kirtland Chardon Road, Willoughby, OH 44094;
440-256-1404
www.lakemetroparks.com/events-activities/activities/cross-country-skiing-
showshoeing

Snowmobiling

Buck Creek State Park
1976 Buck Creek Lane, Springfield, OH 45502; 937-322-5284
parks.ohiodnr.gov/buckcreek

Mosquito Lake State Park
1439 Wilson Sharpsville Road, Cortland, OH 44410; 330-637-2856
parks.ohiodnr.gov/mosquitolake

West Branch State Park, 5570 Esworthy Road, Ravenna, OH 44266; 330-654-4989
parks.ohiodnr.gov/westbranch

Western Reserve Greenway, West 52nd Street and Madison Avenue (Ashtabula) and
North River Road (Warren)
www.traillink.com/trail/western-reserve-greenway/

Ash Cave trail, Hocking Hills

Ohio Renaissance Festival, Waynesburg

Whether your tastes run to music, Renaissance history, or hot air balloons, there's a festival somewhere in Ohio just for you. Wear comfortable shoes, take some cash for the food trucks, and spend a day—or more—soaking up the festival vibe.

FESTIVALS

1 All Ohio Balloon Fest

Union County Airport, 760 Clymer Road, Marysville, OH 43040; 937-243-1091
www.allohioballoonfest.com

You can catch a ride in a hot air balloon at this festival, but those aren't the only rides available. You can choose a tethered balloon ascent, a trip in a biplane, or a helicopter ride. You might even decide on a tandem sky jump. This three-day summertime festival has been going on since 1975, donating all proceeds to the Union County United Way. Balloons you'll see will be every color of the rainbow, and some pretty strange shapes. Balloon flights and glows are scheduled every day of the Fest, and there are always plenty of food vendors and top-flight country music entertainment.

2 Cincinnati Zoo Festival of Lights

3400 Vine Street, Cincinnati, OH 45220; 513-281-4700
cincinnatizoo.org/events/festival-of-lights/

The holidays arrive at the zoo via the Toyland Express and more than 2 million lights. Strolling entertainers roam the zoo through themed areas, like Gingerbread Village, and Fairyland, where there are five hidden fairies. Santa and Mrs. Claus are available for visits. A Wild Lights show is offered at Swan Lake, and there's a black-light Madcap Puppets show. Two S'mores-N-More stands are on the grounds. After Christmas, a Happy ZOO Year party features Father Time and Baby ZOO Year, plus fireworks.

3 Great Trail Arts & Crafts Festival

6331 Canton Road Northwest, Malvern, OH 44644; 330-794-9100
www.greattrailfestival.com

Great Trail is a celebration of Colonial America, with plenty of history on display. There are lectures and demonstrations each day, as well as rendezvous and battle reenactments. The Ohio state tomahawk-throwing contest is part of the action. Entertainment includes flag raisings and parades, fiddlers, cloggers, bands, and pipers. A bison herd, including a white calf born there, is on display at the grounds, as is a scenic grist mill. Crafters who attend for demonstrations and sales include candlemakers, wicker furniture makers, birdhouse builders, soap makers, potters, blacksmiths, and basket makers. There's also a popular Baker's Row.

Jamboree in the Hills

43510 National Road, Belmont, OH 43718; 800-624-5456
www.jamboreeinthehills.com

After 40+ years, "Jambo," as this festival is known, has its own theme song, its own post office, two campground stores, 30 food vendors, and its own emergency ward. Couples are married, babies are born, and families reunite on the grounds. Every morning at 8 o'clock, there's the Redneck Run. It's sort of like the running of the bulls, except it's the running of the diehard country music fans. Holding tight to their 8x10 tarps, festival-goers dash from the starting line to the stage area, snap open the tarps, and claim their spots for the day's musical entertainment. Parties and contests are held early, then concerts run from 4 to 11 p.m. Jambo After Dark runs until 1 a.m., then private parties start all over again. Many concertgoers camp for the week, bringing picnic tables, portable swimming pools, and fire pits to enjoy the music in style. Water and sanitation trucks cruise the campgrounds daily.

Ohioana Book Festival

Ohioana Library, 274 East 1st Avenue, Suite 300, Columbus, OH 43201; 614-466-3831
www.ohioana.org/programs/ohioana-book-festival/

It happens once a year, on a Saturday in April, and it's free. Ohioana is paradise for book lovers, since more than 100 Ohio writers set up shop to sell their wares. You can find everything from history to children's fantasy here, plus all there is in between. There are panel discussions, food trucks, book signing events, and activities for children and teens. For educators, librarians, and workshop directors, the Ohioana Library also provides a directory of authors available for appearances all year long.

Ohio Renaissance Festival

10542 East State Route 73, Waynesville, OH 45068; 513-897-7000
www.renfestival.com

On the grounds of a 30-acre sixteenth-century replica English village, visitors are welcome to Ohio Renaissance on weekends in September and October. Each weekend has its own theme. On Barbarian Invasion Weekend you can try your muscles in strength contests, and then your stomach in eating contests. Traditional Scottish games and music are featured on Highland Weekend, or show your witchy side on Fantasy Weekend. Enter the Men in Tights or the Best Bloomers contests on

Romance Weekend, or renew your wedding vows at the chapel. More than 100 entertainers roam the festival grounds, from acrobats and jugglers to harpists and bagpipers. Sixteenth-century food is available in abundance, like soup in bread bowls, and a pickle cart, plus more ordinary fare, including ice cream and pizza. Handmade crafts, jewelry, and clothing are sold in the Artisan Marketplace.

7 Ohio River Sternwheel Festival

119 Greene Street, Marietta, OH 45750; 740-373-5178
ohioriversternwheelfestival.org

Sternwheeler racing used to be a regular sight along the Ohio River. This festival preserves the tradition. Thousands cheer the boats upriver as whistles blow and captains jockey for position. Other events include the crowning of Queen Genevieve and the Little Miss and Mister, fireworks, a car show, photo contest, and 5K run. There are also children's activities and musical entertainment.

8 Made in Ohio Art & Craft Festival

Hale Farm & Village, 2686 Oak Hill Road, Bath, OH 44210
www.madeinohiofestival.org

Every September, Hale Farm & Village hosts this juried festival of handmade and homegrown products for more than 12,000 visitors. Artisans include woodcarvers, glass and jewelry makers, quilters, artists, potters, and makers of soaps and lotions. Local vintners and brewers are also on hand, plus food vendors. Musical entertainment is provided, and costumed docents are on call throughout the village. At a preview event the night before the festival, there are craft and trade demonstrations, as well as appetizers and beverages.

Shaker Woods Festivals

44337 County Line Road, Columbiana, OH 44408; 330-482-0214
www.shakerwoodsoutdoorexpo.com
www.shakerwoods.com
www.antiquesinthewoods.com
www.christmasinthewoodsohio.com/index.shtml

In the woods behind a farm field off Route 7, four different events make up the Shaker Woods family of festivals. The original Shaker Woods Festival is held over three weekends every August, featuring more than 200 juried craftspeople and artists. Antiques in the Woods is always on a September weekend, featuring dealers in quality antiques and collectibles. The newest event, Shaker Woods Outdoor Expo, takes place at the same time. Outdoor adventurers are invited to meet vendors for hunting, fishing, camping, outdoor art, and outdoor sports. At Christmas in the Woods, during two weekends in October, visitors shop for handcrafted Christmas gifts. All the events include food vendors, themed entertainment, and sometimes extra activities, like poker runs and antique car displays.

Festivals

Harvest time in Ohio

Ever since John Chapman (Johnny Appleseed) scattered his first seeds, Ohioans have loved their apples. We're also famous for grapes, pumpkins, peaches, plums, pears, and berries. From mid-June, when the first strawberries are turning red, to late October, when there's frost on the pumpkins, pickers are covering the fields and orchards to gather in the harvest.

ORCHARDS AND VINEYARDS

A & M Farm Orchard
22141 State Route 251, Midland, OH 45148; 513-875-2500

Apple Hill Orchards
1175 Lexington Ontario Road, Mansfield, OH 44903; 419-884-1500
applehillorchards.com

Beckwith Orchards
1617 Lake Rockwell Road, Kent, OH 44240; 330-673-6433
www.beckwithorchards.com

Branstool Orchards
5895 Johnstown-Utica Road Northeast, Utica, OH 43080; 740-892-3989
branstoolorchards.com

Burnham Orchards
8019 State Route 113, Berlin Heights, OH 44814; 419-588-2138
www.burnhamorchards.com

Cherry Orchards
10340 State Route 669, Crooksville, OH 43731; 740-982-0976

Conine's Country Market
21727 State Route 12, Fostoria, OH 44830; 419-435-9616
coninescountrymarket.com

Fuhrmann Orchards
510 Hansgen Morgan Road, Wheelersburg, OH 45694; 740-776-6406

Hidden Hills Orchard
5680 State Route 26, Marietta, OH 45750; 740-376-9170
www.hiddenhillsorchard.com

Hillcrest Orchards
50336 Telegraph Road, Amherst, OH 44001; 440-965-8884
www.hillcrestfunfarm.com

Legend Hills Orchard and Country Store
11335 Reynolds Road, Utica, OH 43080; 740-892-2498
www.legendhillsorchard.com

MacQueen Orchards
7605 Garden Road, Holland, OH 43528; 419-865-2916
www.macqueenorchards.com

Miller Orchards
8690 Vermilion Road, Amherst, OH 44001; 440-988-8405
millerorchardsltd.com

The Orchard and Co.
7255 US Highway 42, Plain City, OH 43064; 614-873-0510
www.theorchardandcompany.com

Peace Valley Orchards
5667 Adams Road, Rogers, OH 44455; 330-426-9695
www.pvoinc.com

Peifer Orchards
4590 US Highway 68, Yellow Springs, OH 45387; 937-767-2208
www.peiferorchards.com

Rittman Orchards
13548 Mt. Eaton Road North, Doylestown, OH 44230; 330-925-4152
rittmanorchards.com

Scenic Ridge Fruit Farms
2031 State Route 89, Jeromesville, OH 44840; 419-368-3353
www.baumanorchards.com/locations/scenic-ridge/

Ohio vineyard

At a Cincinnati Reds game

Ohio is the proud home of two Major League baseball clubs: the historic Cincinnati Reds (baseball's oldest club) and the Cleveland Indians. And with Cleveland Browns, the Cincinnati Bengals and the Pro Football Hall of Fame in Canton, we're pretty big fans of football too. But Ohioans are also partial to other sports. Besides basketball, hockey, soccer, lacrosse, and rugby, we're big roller derby fans.

SPORTS

Pro Football Hall of Fame

2121 George Halas Drive Northwest, Canton, OH 44708; 330-456-8207
www.profootballhof.com

For football fans, it's an emotional moment to stand in the Hall of Fame Gallery among the bronze busts of legendary players. That's only the beginning of the Hall of Fame experience, though. Many of the most iconic, historic times experienced by those Hall of Fame heroes are chronicled in the Moments, Memories & Mementos Gallery. The Lamar Hunt Super Bowl Gallery and its Super Bowl Theater use interactive displays, film, and mementos to call each Super Bowl game back to life. There are also exhibits devoted to officiating, and to other football leagues. Elsewhere in the museum, interactive video and trivia games entertain and test visitors' skills. Annual events held at the museum include the two-week Enshrinement Festival celebrating new inductees. Additionally, every year prior to the NFL season, a Hall of Fame exhibition game is played at Fawcett Stadium. The Hall of Fame also maintains an eight-field sports complex for football, lacrosse, and soccer events.

Baseball

Cincinnati Reds—Great American Ball Park

100 Joe Nuxhall Way, Cincinnati, OH 45202; 513-765-7000
www.mlb.com/reds/ballpark

Cleveland Indians—Progressive Field

2401 Ontario Street, Cleveland, OH 44115; 216-420-HITS (4487)
www.mlb.com/indians/ballpark

Akron Rubber Ducks—Canal Park

300 South Main Street, Akron, OH 44308; 330-253-5151 or 855-97-QUACK (78225)
www.milb.com/content/page.jsp?ymd=20121127&content_
id=40427710&sid=t402&vkey=team1

Columbus Clippers—Huntington Park

330 Huntington Park Lane, Columbus, OH 43215; 614-462-5250 or Ticket Line:
614-462-2757
www.milb.com/index.jsp?sid=t445

Dayton Dragons—Fifth Third Field

220 North Patterson Boulevard, Dayton, OH 45402; 937-228-BATS (2287)
www.milb.com/index.jsp?sid=t459

Toledo Mud Hens—Fifth Third Field

406 Washington Street, Toledo, OH 43604; 419-725-HENS (4367)
www.milb.com/index.jsp?sid=t512

Lake County Captains—Classic Park

35300 Vine Street, Eastlake, OH 44095; 440-975-8085
www.milb.com/index.jsp?sid=t437

Lake Erie Crushers—Sprenger Stadium

2009 Baseball Boulevard, Avon, OH 44011; 440-934-3636
lakeeriecrushers.com/landing/index

Mahoning Valley Scrappers—Eastwood Field

111 Eastwood Mall Boulevard, Niles, OH 44446-1357; 330-505-0000
www.milb.com/index.jsp?sid=t545

Basketball

Cleveland Cavaliers—Quicken Loans Arena

One Center Court, Cleveland, OH 44115; 216-420-2000 or Ticket Line: 800-820-CAVS (2287)
www.nba.com/cavaliers/

Football

Cincinnati Bengals—Paul Brown Stadium

One Paul Brown Stadium, Cincinnati, OH 45202; Ticket Line: 513-621-8383 or
866-621-8383
www.bengals.com

Cleveland Browns—First Energy Stadium

100 Alfred Lerner Way, Cleveland, OH 44114; 440-824-3434
www.clevelandbrowns.com

Hockey

Columbus Blue Jackets—Nationwide Arena

200 West Nationwide Boulevard, Columbus, OH 43215; 614-246-3350
www.nhl.com/bluejackets/arena/home

Lacrosse

Ohio Machine—Fortress Obetz
1841 Williams Road, Columbus, OH 43207; 614-754-1973
www.theohiomachine.com

Roller Derby

Burning River Roller Derby, Cleveland
www.burningriverderby.com

Central Ohio Roller Derby, Mount Vernon
www.centralohiorollerderby.com

Gem City Roller Derby, Dayton
www.gemcityrollerderby.com

Glass City Rollers, Toledo
glasscityrollers.com

Ohio Valley Roller Girls, St. Clairsville
www.ohiovalleyrollergirls.com

Soccer

Columbus Crew SC–MAPFRE Stadium
One Black and Gold Boulevard, Columbus, OH 43211; 614-447-4169
www.columbuscrewsc.com

Ohio State Reformatory, Mansfield

Every state has its own strange, out-of-the-way corners, where a worthwhile bit of history might be recalled, or a unique piece of art stands without apology. Or it might just be a fun place to go for a day trip.

ODDS AND ENDS

STANDARD FAMILY SIZE
GALVANIZED

Washboards like this were, and still are, made at the Columbus Washboard Factory

1 Annie Oakley, Frank Butler Gravesites

Brock Cemetery, 11775-11791 Greenville Saint Marys Road, Versailles, OH 45380
www.findagrave.com/memorial/774
www.atlasobscura.com/places/annie-oakleys-grave

Signs leading to Brock Cemetery are present on more than one road in the area, and an Ohio Historical Marker stands with the gravestones, which simply read, "At Rest." The couple, who were married 50 years, died within weeks of each other. Rumor has it that Annie's cremains are actually preserved in one of her trophies inside Butler's coffin. Annie Oakley, who beat sharpshooter Frank Butler in a shooting contest when she was 15, then married him a year later, was born near Versailles. Her father taught her to shoot, and she later supported her mother and siblings by hunting after her father died. She and Butler became stars of Buffalo Bill's Wild West Show in 1885, and were world famous. Oakley was a champion for women's rights, and once volunteered a company of 50 female sharpshooters to President William McKinley for the Spanish-American War.

2 b.a. Sweetie Candy Company

6770 Brookpark Road, Cleveland, OH 44129; 216-739-2244
www.sweetiescandy.com

An incredible 400,000 pounds of candy, in 40,000 square feet, are for sale at Sweetie's, which calls itself the largest candy store in America. You can buy candy by the piece, by the scoop, or by the bag. Do you need 30 pounds? They sell master cases, just for people like you. Sweetie's does a lot of wholesale candy sales too, which accounts for those master cases. You could overdose on sugar just by walking down the long aisles of candy racks. Jelly Belly, Godiva, Haribo, Hershey, M&M, Pez, Tootsie Rolls, Wrigley, and more are all here. You can even find old-fashioned names like Necco and Slo-Poke and Chiclets. There's also a Sweeties Soda Shoppe that seats 150, with 36 flavors of ice cream made on-site. What else is there to say? Mmmmmmmmm!

Columbus Washboard Factory

14 Gallagher Avenue, Logan, OH 43138; 740-380-3828
columbuswashboard.com

Touring a washboard factory might not be high on your day trip wish list, but give it a chance—you get a free refrigerator magnet with every tour, after all. Here you'll see some of the company's original manufacturing equipment in daily use. Each washboard is still made mostly by hand, one at a time. The surfaces of the boards can be spiral metal, galvanized, stainless steel, brass, glass, cork, chalk, or mirror. You can use them for handwashing at home, in camp, or while deployed to the Middle East. They're very popular for decorative use. Oh, you can also use them to play bluegrass music, especially at the annual Washboard Musical Festival held Father's Day weekend in Logan. Musical washboards come in many sizes, shapes, and materials and can even be fashioned in guitar shapes. The factory store also sells soaps and salves, laundry items like drying racks, craft supplies, Fostoria glassware, and New Zealand butter.

Cornhenge

4995 Rings Road, Dublin, OH 43017; 614-410-4550
www.visitdublinohio.com/things-to-do/attractions/art-in-public-places/
www.atlasobscura.com/places/cornhenge

The official name is *Field of Corn (with Osage Orange Trees)*. Locals reportedly call it the "see-ment corn," and they're actually right. These are six-foot sculptures of ears of corn, made of white concrete, rising right out of the ground in tidy rows. There are 109 ears of corn, in four slightly different shapes. The installation was commissioned by the Dublin Arts Council in 1995 to honor a local farmer, Sam Frantz, who developed several hybrid corn varieties. The Osage orange trees, by the way, are off in one corner of the field. Cornhenge, as it is commonly known, was not a popular art installation at first, but people have come to appreciate it. The site gets a lot of visitors, and weddings have even been held there.

House of Trash

Blue Rock Station, 1190 Virginia Ridge Road, Philo, OH 43771; 740-674-4300
www.bluerockstation.com

Jay and Annie Warmke started building what they call the Earthship in 1996 and have lived in it since 2004. Starting with 1,200 tires brought from an illegal dump, they rammed the tires full of dirt and used them to construct the walls of the house. Other walls, both in the main house and in outbuildings, are built of straw bales, reclaimed wood, glass and plastic bottles, or aluminum cans. The couple's goal in building the Earthship was to combine engineering, art, and recycling as part of sustainable practice. They also use solar collectors and rainwater collectors. Because so many people have expressed interest in their project, the Warmkes host Saturday tour days several times a year (see website for dates), conduct regular workshops in sustainable living, and accept interns who live and work on the property.

6 The J. M. Smucker Company Store and Café

333 Wadsworth Road, Orrville, OH 44667; 330-684-1500
www.jmsmucker.com/smuckers-corporate/smuckers-store-orrville

In a nod to its founding as a cider mill, the entry to Smucker's Store and Café is lined by apple trees. Inside the sprawling store you can find all their products, arranged in sections. Besides the Smucker's brand of jams and jellies, they produce Dickinson's fruit spreads and other familiar names like Jif, Crisco, Hungry Jack, Pillsbury (yes, you can buy a Doughboy), Dunkin Donuts Coffee, and much more. They also manufacture pet foods. After shopping, you can eat in the café, which features their own products, of course, and entrées baked in a wood-fired oven. If you have any room left after the meal, make your own sundae at the Sundae Shop.

7 Longaberger Basket Building

1500 East Main Street, Newark, OH 43055-8847

It's been a roadside icon in Ohio since it was built in 1997—the seven-story building that looks like a market basket. It was the headquarters of the Longaberger Company, which sold pricey handmade baskets through direct sales at home parties. After the founder's death, the company was sold and the building eventually abandoned when employees were moved to other quarters. Though the property has been sadly neglected, restoration plans are being made by a new owner.

Ohio State Reformatory

100 Reformatory Road, Mansfield, OH 44905; 419-522-2644
www.mrps.org

You can take a self-guided tour of the former state prison, but who would want to? It's much safer, given the reformatory's dark history and reputation for ghosts, to join a tour group. There are several guided tours from which to choose, including one led by a former inmate (for mature audiences only). Since the reformatory was famously used to film *The Shawshank Redemption*, you can also follow the Shawshank Trail from the reformatory to 14 filming sites in and around Mansfield, marked by handy "Movie Site" posters. Special events held at the reformatory include a murder mystery dinner theater, a fun run, charity events, and a tattoo festival. A local vintage baseball team, the Mansfield Independents, plays home games there. Dinners for conferences and fundraisers for up to 400 can be arranged, though they don't allow weddings or receptions.

Piatt Castles

Mac-A-Cheek Castle: 10051 Township Road 47, West Liberty, OH 43357
Mac-O-Chee Castle: 2319 State Route 287, West Liberty, OH 43357; 937-465-2821
www.piattcastles.org

The seventh generation of Piatts keeps these elaborate homes, built in the late 1800s, as repositories of history, and also as object lessons for the importance of family history. They try to make tours "less about us" and more about the visitors' own family stories and mementos. The castles are open April through October for tours of artifacts, photographs, period furnishings, and exhibits. Their nonprofit foundation provides multiple educational programs for students, focusing on Ohio history, geology, literature, math, and architecture through projects, crafts, games, storytelling, and theater. There are also camps every summer that feature the castles as springboards for imagination and theater.

Saltpetre Cave State Nature Preserve

Near Hocking Hills State Park, 19852 State Route 664, Logan, OH 43138; 614-265-6561
naturepreserves.ohiodnr.gov/saltpetrecave
Permit application: naturepreserves.ohiodnr.gov/Portals/0/Forms/dnap/permits/ApplicationAccessPermit.pdf

One of the best-kept secrets of the ODNR is this seldom-visited nature preserve in the middle of a busy tourist area; access is only available with a permit (apply at least 14 days in advance). The recess caves here are named for the potassium nitrate, or saltpetre, that was once mined for gunpowder manufacture. They are located on 14 acres with

a short trail system providing access. Saltpetre is still visible on some of the cave ceilings. A couple of the caves are more than a hundred feet deep. You'll need to bring a flashlight along and watch your footing to get all the way inside them.

11 Smith Cemetery State Nature Preserve

4400 Boyd Road, Plain City, OH 43064; 614-265-6561
naturepreserves.ohiodnr.gov/smithcemetery

The wet and swampy Darby Plains around Smith Cemetery were considered good only for wildflowers and bur oaks by early settlers, who bypassed the area quickly while swatting at clouds of mosquitoes. Farmers from New England eventually drained the plains for cropland and obliterated much of the tallgrass prairie. Soon the original flora survived mostly in tiny family cemeteries like this one, donated to the state in the early 1800s by Samuel Smith Jr. The site is less than an acre in area but is very much worth a short visit to commune with the ghosts of long-vanished pioneers.

12 Spangler Candy Store and Museum

400 North Portland Street, Bryan, OH 43506; 888-636-4221 or 419-633-6439
www.spanglercandy.com

It's disappointing that you can't actually tour the kitchens here because of FDA regulations, but the Dum Dums Trolley can take you everywhere else in the Spangler complex. This is the home of a candy you've known and loved all your life, beginning with Saf-T-Pops. They also make Dum Dums lollipops (12 million per day), Spangler Candy Canes (2.7 million per day), and Spangler Circus Peanuts. Plus (who knew?), they make Goetze Cow Tales in three different flavors. At the museum, you can see a historical timeline and artifacts, taste product samples, and watch a film showing how candy is made. School tours are offered and include curriculum-based worksheets.

3 Thurber House

77 Jefferson Avenue, Columbus, OH 43215; 614-464-1032
www.thurberhouse.org

Visitors to the museum are encouraged to consider themselves guests of the Thurber family in some of the rooms. You can sit on the furniture, play the piano, and be comfortably at home. Two floors contain period furnishings, family items, and Thurber memorabilia. On the third floor is an apartment reserved for visiting writers and artists. Outdoors, a reading garden includes statues inspired by Thurber cartoons. The house is open for free self-guided tours every afternoon; guided tours for a small fee are available on Sunday afternoons or by special appointment. Programs at Thurber House include adult and youth writing programs, author residencies, and resources for writers.

4 USS *Cod* Submarine Memorial

1201 North Marginal Road, Cleveland, OH 44114; 216-566-8770
www.usscod.org

The *Cod* is a remarkable example of World War II diesel submarines. It sank the Japanese destroyer *Karukaya* in 1944, and effected the only international submarine-to-submarine rescue in history when in 1945 it rescued the crew of Dutch submarine *O-19*, which was grounded on a reef. On the day we toured the *Cod*, one of our group was wildly excited to discover it was nearly identical to the one on which he'd served. Some 30 years and maybe 100 pounds after his tour of duty, Dick dove through hatches and navigated ladders like the 19-year-old bubblehead he used to be. Soon Dick was leading a large group of tourists through the spaces he'd known intimately. He showed off his torpedo room bunk, his cramped workspace, and the crew mess that could seat 24 if everyone kept their elbows tucked. Your tour might not be as personal, but you'll enjoy it just as much. The *Cod* is open May through September.

Odds and Ends

Index *(entries followed by a "p" indicate photographs highlighting the entry)*

About the Author

Cathy Hester Seckman is a lifelong resident of East Liverpool, Ohio, and has been a fan of day trips since her parents first said, "Let's take a ride!" on a Sunday afternoon. Writing this book has been an adventure as she discovers new favorite places and revisits old ones.

Seckman is a back-of-the-book indexer, and has written some 160 indexes, including the one in this book. She has published more than a dozen short stories, hundreds of magazine articles, and thousands of newspaper articles. She is the author of *East Liverpool*, an Images of America title released by Arcadia Publishing in 2015. *Weirdo World*, her young adult fantasy novel, was published by Cool Well Press in 2012. As an indie author, she cowrote *Bad Moon Rising*, a murder mystery set between Woodstock and the Kent State shootings; *Secrets Matter*, a women's fiction title; and an anthology, *H2O Mysteries*.